WAR AND PACIFISM

The Facts and the Choices

by
Margaret Cooling

Scripture Union
130 City Road, London EC1V 2NJ

© 1988 Margaret Cooling

First published 1988
by Scripture Union, 130 City Road, London EC1V 2NJ

ISBN 0 86201 389 5

Illustrations: Trevor Waugh
Design: Tony Contale Graphics

Phototypeset by Input Typesetting Ltd., London SW19 8DR.
Printed and bound in Great Britain by Ebenezer Baylis & Son Ltd.,
Worcester.

CONTENTS

TO THE LEADER

THE AIM
This book does not provide a detailed discussion of war and pacifism as there are many excellent books available that cover this subject. Some of those which the leader will find useful are listed at the back. The aim of this book is to look at some of the *principles* involved in the subject and to give young people the skills they need in order to handle information about war, which can often look both frightening and confusing if it is just presented as a series of cold facts.

LEADERSHIP
The material is presented with the needs of the youth group leader in mind. Instructions are given as to how best to organize the activities and times of discussion, and the text speaks in places as the leader would address the group. This is designed to help less experienced leaders to develop ways of communicating with their group. It is therefore quite possible for members of the group to share in the leadership.

HANDLING MATERIAL
Each unit contains a mix of information, activities, biblical material and 'comment'. The *information* gives the group a basis from which to start their thinking. The *activities* demonstrate what is involved in the basic issues looked at. The *biblical material* comes with a certain amount of comment which may be useful in guiding discussions or in developing other questions for discussion. The sections marked '*Think about it . . .*' are for reflection. They raise issues the group may not have thought about before, or help to take their thinking further.

SELECTING MATERIAL
The units are grouped together as displayed on the contents page but they don't have to be dealt with in this order; they can be changed to suit your group's needs and your particular situation. You may, for example, feel that you want to deal with some practical options nearer the beginning rather than waiting until the last units. One alternative arrangement is outlined on page 00. Some units are more vital than others and you may feel able to leave some out, but please be cautious about leaving out the material on choices and the use of the Bible unless your group is very sure about these subjects.

THE PASTORAL ELEMENT
When studying a topic as difficult as this it is important to remember the pastoral element in youth work. Many teenagers feel very threatened by this subject and it is important to balance its seriousness with hope. *Every* unit should contain a positive

message and not leave the group with a feeling of despair. If you rearrange them, see that the positive and negative are kept in balance. This is particularly important in the first unit as it is necessary to state the full force of the problem before a group can begin to look for answers. If you feel that members of your group may have difficulty coping with the subject, please use the section on hope at the beginning, rather than at the end.

ACTIVITIES

There are activities at each stage of the units. These are not just to 'liven up' a youth group; they are integral to the teaching process. In some cases activities will have to be omitted if time is short but this should not be a general rule. This book uses active learning methods throughout and is based on the philosophy that people learn best when they are involved at more than a purely verbal level. Time needs to be made for the activities and they need to be prepared carefully. It is important that the group sees them as something more than the trimmings.

THE ISSUE

Throughout this book, war has not been rigidly distinguished from nuclear war. They *are* separate issues in that nuclear war contains completely new concepts concerning the scale and type of war, but they are also closely related. Any nuclear state going to war has to bear in mind the possibility of escalation; this is probably the reason the 'superpowers' have not directly fought each other since World War Two. People have always been able to kill each other in large numbers and although, for other reasons, nuclear weapons stand in a class of their own, they can be seen as part of the long evolution of weaponry. *No* war can be fought now by any of the nuclear states, no intervention in someone else's war can be contemplated, without the ghost of the mushroom cloud haunting the decision-makers.

AN ALTERNATIVE STRUCTURE

1 FACING THE ISSUES
1.1 Problems
1.2 Hope

2 MAKING DECISIONS
2.1 Choices
2.2 Using the Bible

3 LOVE IS . . .

4 PEACE AND WAR
4.1 What is peace?
4.2 Why does war happen?

5 WAR AND WEAPONS
5.1 Taming the tiger
5.2 The facts of life

6 JUSTICE AND THE JUST WAR
6.1 The rules of the game
6.2 The nuclear umbrella

7 FACING UP TO SIN AND EVIL
7.1 Getting what you deserve
7.2 You hit me and I'll hit you back

8 THE STATE AND THE USE OF FORCE
8.1 Big brother
8.2 Power, authority, force and violence

9 OPTIONS
9.1 Counting the cost
9.2 Practical options
9.3 Waging peace

Note: Section 9 could be done over two weeks.

1
PROBLEMS AND CHOICES

1.1 PROBLEMS

You've got problems even if you don't know it, for the subject you are about to study is fraught with difficulties. In this first session we are only going to look at the problems, later we will look at the various responses to them.

ACTIVITY ONE

Complacency

Stand one person in the middle of the room on a piece of paper labelled COMPLACENCY. Below are a few of the thoughts about this subject which might shake that person out of their lethargy.

Write each of the statements on a piece of paper, put them in a bowl, mix them up and ask the rest of the group to pull out one piece of paper at a time. As each person reads out their statement they can give the person standing on the paper a gentle push so that they step off their paper labelled COMPLACENCY.

This can be arranged instead as a tug of war. Stand a person on the piece of paper labelled COMPLACENCY, as before, but ask them to hold the centre of a rope. Label the two ends of the rope PACIFISM and INVOLVEMENT IN WAR. As each person pulls their piece of paper out of the 'hat' they have to decide which end of the rope to take up on the basis of the comment on their piece of paper. As they take up the rope they can give it a gentle pull or they can wait until everybody has selected which end of the rope they join and then have a tug of war.

STATEMENTS

1 You couldn't live with yourself if you killed someone.

2 Jesus said 'love your enemies'; killing them is hardly loving them.

3 Life and death are matters for God to decide, not us. We object to abortion and euthanasia, war is no different.

4 Dropping a bomb on the enemy would wipe out many Christians.

5 We should try to apply Jesus' teaching to the state and not keep it just for personal relationships.

6 There are enough weapons to kill us many times; isn't once enough?

7 We can't be sure there will not be a mistake. No human being or computer should be in charge of such destructive weapons.

8 There would be no victors in a nuclear war; we would all be losers.

9 Wars breed other wars; war in itself is never a solution.

10 We could feed the starving with what we spend on arms.

11 Even if the state can wage war, that doesn't mean a Christian should help it in its dirty work.

12 For the first three hundred years after Christ, Christians were pacifists. We should follow their example.

13 Is anything worth killing for?

14 All through the Bible there is a strong emphasis on 'power in weakness'; Christians shouldn't be involved in the worldly use of power.

15 You wouldn't be able to forgive yourself for not resisting evil and so allowing people to die.

16 Some things are so valuable that they are worth dying for.

17 War is a means of judgment in the Old Testament; some evil nations still need judging in this way. We punish thugs at home, why not punish international thugs?

18 In the Old Testament God allowed war. Has he changed his mind?

19 God gave states the power of the sword (Romans 13:1–7) and meant them to use it. A national boundary shouldn't stop right being enforced.

20 Doesn't justice sometimes need enforcing?

21 More innocent people die in peace time than in war. The oppressed should be defended.

22 Life is not totally sacred in the Bible; it could be forfeited, there was a death penalty.

23 Abandoning nuclear weapons is an open invitation to an aggressor. To disarm would be irresponsible.

24 We can't 'dis-invent' nuclear weapons; we must therefore exercise some responsibility towards them.

25 The Sermon on the Mount was meant for personal relationships, not politics. You can't apply 'love your enemies' to the political realm.

26 We have to take evil very seriously; weapons are one way of keeping it under control.

27 We live in a sinful world; there will always be wars. All people can do is try to reduce the evil, not abolish it.

28 Images taken from war are used in the Bible to teach good things: we are told to wage spiritual warfare like dedicated soldiers; the end of the world is described as a battle; when Jesus comes again it will not be as a baby but as the one who conquers evil; soldiers who are converted are not told to desert.

As you can see, this is not an easy subject. There are no slick answers, no easy solutions, no comfortable options. Until you have first understood the problems you cannot begin to look for any sort of answers.

ALTERNATIVE ACTIVITIES

1 If you have not got the space to try the activity above, try the following. Draw around one member of the group while they lie down on a large sheet of paper. Cut out the shape and carefully tear it in two. Label one half 'war' and the other 'peace'. Everybody in the group should write down on appropriate sides of the 'person' the sort of problems and doubts that leave people feeling 'torn in two'. Look at the previous list to help if you get stuck.

2 If you have room, put a large piece of paper on the wall with *Blu-Tak*. Put a few

marks on it to resemble bricks and ask everyone to write 'war and peace graffiti' on the wall, trying to top each other's graffiti.

Think about it . . .
This often looks a dreadfully depressing subject, which it is; but for the Christian the certainty that God is in control brings hope into the situation. The Bible makes it clear that one day wars will be no more.

• Look up Revelation 21:1–4.
This passage talks about the Christian hope: at the end of time, evil will finally be judged and defeated and 'the Prince of peace' will reign. Peace won't come by human effort but by the direct intervention of God. As this hope relies on God rather than on humanity, it is a hope that is certain, not a vague possibility. In the meantime, Christians are called to work in partnership with God for a form of peace in this world.

1.2 CHOICES

We have had a very brief look at the problem. Before we can start looking at the answers we need to see how we make decisions, because this session will involve us all in a decision-making process of some sort. Actually, we are always making decisions; we have to decide about friends and jobs, about actions and attitudes.

ACTIVITY ONE

Ways of choosing
Below are two lists: the different types of things people choose, and the various methods of choosing. Write the choices on separate pieces of paper and put them in a hat. Write the methods of choosing on separate pieces of paper (preferably of a different colour to the choices) and place them in a different hat. Pass round both hats so that each person taking part gets two pieces of paper. If there are more than twelve people in the group the activity can be done in pairs. Each person has to read out what is on their piece(s) of

paper. For example:

Choice: Which breakfast cereal to eat.
Method: Look at the consequences.

In each case the person has to say whether or not the method of choice is appropriate in that particular case, and give reasons for their answer.

CHOICES
1 Which breakfast cereal to eat.
2 Choosing a boyfriend/girlfriend.
3 What clothes to wear.
4 Who to marry.
5 Which programme to watch on television.
6 Where to go on holiday.

7 Who starts a game first.

8 Who will rule the country.

9 What you will do when you leave school.

10 Whether to join the armed forces.

11 Whether to tell a lie.

12 Whether to commit a murder.

METHODS

1 Vote.

2 Look at the situation and weigh up the 'pros' and the 'cons'.

3 Look at the consequences for yourself and for others.

4 Refuse to decide.

5 Look at your own likes and dislikes.

6 Discuss it with others.

7 Use your own conscience.

8 Flip a coin or draw lots.

9 Do as your parents, the school or the state says.

10 Decide what would cause the greatest happiness for the greatest number of people.

11 Do what everybody else is doing.

12 Go by what God has said about it.

Listen carefully to the answers people give. Is there any sort of pattern emerging? Do people use different ways of choosing for different things? Does the method of choice alter when it affects people personally?

Think about it . . .

We are all making decisions all of the time. Many people don't stop to think how they make those decisions. With a subject as difficult and as important as war and pacifism we need to stop and look at the process of coming to a decision, rather than just react to the material we are presented with.

For example, many people just react against war when faced with its horrors, without stopping to think about the horrors of unchecked aggression. Others endorse our present weapons systems for practical reasons, without considering whether they are morally right or wrong.

CHECK OUT THE BIBLE

In the Bible choice is seen as something that is given to humanity. People have freedom of choice to accept God or reject him. People can choose right or wrong. This gift of freedom of choice carries with it great responsibility: people are held to be responsible for their actions, one day having to answer to God for them. Look up the following passages, then think and talk about the questions.

● Genesis 3:1–7

What are the advantages of being able to choose between good and evil? What are the disadvantages?

● Joshua 24:14–15

Life is full of decisions – some trivial and some very important. How do some people try to avoid making decisions?

● Matthew 25:31–46

Decisions have to be answered for; God holds people responsible for their actions. How would life be different if we never had to answer to God for our behaviour? Would we behave differently if we never had to suffer the results of our actions?

MAKING DECISIONS

People tend to make decisions in one of three ways:

1 Refuse to make a decision

Some people simply refuse to decide! They let things happen in a random way, or follow what everybody else is doing.

Problem

This makes for a rather chaotic life. It leaves the 'decision-makers' the victims of circumstance; they are exercising no control over what is happening to them. Not making a decision is in fact a form of decision-making; you are still responsible *for having let things happen.*

2 Look at consequences and aim for the greatest happiness

The second way of choosing is the one most commonly used. Most people have a rough and ready 'rule of thumb' over what is right and what is wrong. But when they have to make a moral choice they look at the situation and weigh things up, taking into consideration the consequences and what would cause the greatest happiness for the most people.

Problems

There are several problems with this. First of all it puts an awful lot of responsibility on the person who is making the decision; they have to decide what 'right' means and what 'wrong' means *in each situation.*

Secondly, whether something is 'right' or 'wrong' also depends on the consequences – which are often very difficult to calculate. Consequences can form a chain reaction that goes on for years; we can never *fully* know them.

To demonstrate this, make a simple statement to the person sitting next to you; for instance, 'I kicked the dog'. Ask them to add what happened next. This goes on all around the room, each person adding a consequence to the statement of the person before them, until you have a long 'chain reaction' of consequences.

This is an extreme example but it makes the point that consequences are, in the long term, unpredictable. We need to take consequences into account to help in our decision-making, but we cannot pin all our morality on them.

Thirdly, this form of decision-making relies on knowing what is the greatest happiness. What makes *me* happy might not make *you* happy! Do we mean long-term or short-term happiness? Whose measure of happiness are we going to use? It would make some of my pupils happy if they passed their school exams, but many of them are lazy. If I shot the laziest pupil I would motivate the others to work and thus achieve their greatest happiness by helping them pass their exams.

Most of us have a sneaking feeling that shooting pupils is wrong! The greatest happiness of the greatest number is not enough on its own, for it allows you to do things to the minority that would make them more than unhappy.

3 Obey an authority

The final way of making a decision is to use some outside authority, such as:

• Parents. Unfortunately parents are not infallible.

• The state. The state can tell people to do things that are immoral; one glance at Nazi Germany should be enough to demonstrate this.

• Religion. This is probably the authority which has most influence on people's moral decisions – not only for the Christian, but for many 'religious' people.

Problems

Firstly, moral rules can seem rigid and unbending, making no allowance for the different circumstances in which people find themselves. However, this does mean that right and wrong are not up to each individual to decide, neither do they change as political fashions change. In the Bible certain things are right or wrong 'of themselves', not because of the consequences or because of the happiness or unhappiness that they cause. Right and wrong are decided by the character of God.

Secondly, it is sometimes difficult to see how to apply general 'rules' in a complex situation. People can know what is right and wrong in broad terms, but they would not deny that there are problems in applying such principles in our modern world. Sometimes people find themselves in difficult situations where they have to make a choice and *none* of the options open to them is what they would label 'right'. In such situations Christians still have to choose, and then they often have to bring in other methods of coming to a decision.

It is important, in a situation where a person has to choose between two wrongs, not to label a wrong as a right.

Right and wrong need to be firmly distinguished. For example, if a murderer is looking for a victim, do you point him in the right direction or do you lie? Either way you have to bear some guilt, for both are wrong actions. At this point Christians start looking at things such as consequences to help them in their decision-making, but they do not use them actually to define what is right or wrong.

ACTIVITY TWO

(This activity may be omitted if time is short).

The week after

The scene: There are thirty of you; you are the survivors of a nuclear attack on your country. Your group is largely female, all of them are of child-bearing age. You are living in a remote part of Scotland where the contamination is minimal but so are the food supplies. You have a few sheep and cattle, you can fish in the loch and may be able to grow some crops in the valley. Take it from here . . .

1 How do you organize your community? Do you need a leader or a means of coming to group decisions?
2 How do you organize work?
3 Make a short-list of rules (right and wrong) for your community.
4 You discover some old Bibles in the ruins of a church. On the one hand, the Bibles state quite plainly that you should not commit adultery; on the other hand, God made it plain to both Adam and Noah that he wanted life to go on and the world to be populated. If you stick to the ruling on adultery, most of the women will not have children. What are you going to do?

- Look at the rules of your community. Do they conflict with the Bible's rules?
- Are there areas where it is difficult to apply the Bible to your situation, either because there is more than one requirement or because your situation is not directly covered in the Bible?
- Pass a judgment on your own rules (using the Bible's standards). For each one decide whether they are . . .

1 Good
2 Lesser good (under the circumstances)
3 Lesser wrong (under the circumstances)
4 Wrong

CHECK OUT THE BIBLE

The Bible defines what is right and what is wrong, by looking at the character of God. Right things reflect what God is or does; wrong things describe everything he isn't, or wouldn't do. But the Bible is not a text book giving a ready-made answer to every question. The Bible has to be used carefully and with thought and effort. There were no nuclear weapons in biblical times so we can't look up texts on them and hope for a straight yes/no answer. Instead the timeless truths of the Bible have to be applied to our own complex situation. When talking about modern war we stand on the very borderline of decision-making, trying to apply biblical principles to a difficult modern issue. By the end of this book many of you may have come to different conclusions from each other, but *that will not be because there is no such thing as right or wrong* in this issue. People differ about *how* the *right end* of peace is to be achieved.

2
USING THE BIBLE

When making decisions, Christians use the Bible. It is not the only way they make decisions; it is used in conjunction with the Holy Spirit, the Christian's conscience and the Christian community. This does not mean the Bible is overruled, rather the Holy Spirit and other Christians help us understand what the Bible is saying.

The Bible is not an easy book, and in this section we will be looking at how to use it.

ACTIVITY ONE

Antiques road show

Each person in the group should bring in something 'old fashioned' and explain to the rest of the group what it is or does. The others need to pass a judgment on the object, saying whether it is:

a. Still useful in some way
b. Definitely useful and valuable
c. Timeless (will remain useful)
d. Obsolete

For example:
Object: A slide rule
Judgment: Obsolete

Think about it . . .

Our society is moving very rapidly and things quickly go out of date. Today's inventions will lie on tomorrow's scrap heap. We are used to rapid change and don't expect things to remain the same. This makes it difficult to understand the unchanging nature of God and the unchanging nature of the Bible.

The truths contained in the Bible can be applied to any age. It is not a dead book from the past but, for the Christian, part of a living relationship. The Bible deals with things that don't change: the nature of God and the nature of people. Although our environment changes, our basic make-up doesn't.

CHECK OUT THE BIBLE

Look up these two references, and discuss the questions:

● Hebrews 13:8
What does it mean to say that God is unchanging?

● Matthew 5:17–18
Jesus said the laws that God had given would not change; right and wrong are established for good. Do you think that is unnecessarily rigid?

ACTIVITY TWO

How not to use the Bible

You will need small pieces of cardboard (the size of a file card), some pencils and an old cardboard box. Make two slits in the box, big enough to post the pieces of card through. Label one slit 'questions' and the other slit 'answers'.

Elect several members of the group to act as the memory bank of a computer. Place the cardboard box in front of them.

The rest of the group should write questions on the cards and post them one at a time through the 'questions' slit. The 'memory bank' should produce an answer to each question and post it back through the 'answer' slit.

Answers should be kept short and

preferably one word: Yes, No, Sometimes, Usually. For example:

Question: Is it right to drink alcohol?
Answer: Sometimes.

ACTIVITY THREE

Pin sticking

In groups, try opening the Bible at random and sticking in a pin. Give your verse to the group next to you. Each group has to think up a situation for which that verse could have been the guidance. For example:

Isaiah 14:11: 'Maggots are spread out beneath you and worms cover you.'
Situation: I was wondering whether to skip church and go fishing, and I opened my Bible at Isaiah 14:11 and decided that it was right for me to go fishing.

Think about it . . .

These are just two examples of how not to use the Bible. It is not an answer book nor is it a religious game of chance. Of course God can use anything but that is not how he normally works. The Bible is meant to be read as a whole. If you select bits at random, or just try to look up 'answers' without putting them in context, you can make the Bible say anything! The Bible gives straight answers on basic issues of right and wrong but, in situations that the Bible doesn't cover, the general principles of right and wrong have to be applied to the new situation.

SOME HINTS ON USING THE BIBLE

1 The Bible was written to help us find, and maintain, an active relationship with God; it is not just for problem-solving.
Look up Hebrews 4:12–13. What words and phrases suggest this?

The Bible was not written to give us a set of instructions *instead* of a relationship with God; it was never meant to be just a 'book of rules'. The rules that *are* there are to show us what God is like and how to relate to him.

2 The Bible is meant to be read as a whole; individual parts should be read in context. Both Old and New Testaments are important for Christians.
Look up 2 Timothy 3:15–17. What important functions does it have?

The Bible is not there to pick and

▶▶

▶▶

choose from, ignoring the bits you don't like! Rather, a person should be open to being changed by the teaching of the whole Bible.

3 If there is a verse which is difficult to understand, a more straightforward statement somewhere else in the Bible will often help to clarify it.
The Bible is not an easy book, a fact that it admits itself! See 2 Peter 3:14–16.

Don't worry if you do not understand parts of the Bible; most people are in the same position. It's not like a comic; understanding the Bible requires work, thought and prayer.

4 The New Testament is used to clarify the Old Testament, and not the other way round. Jesus is regarded by Christians as the last word on a subject.
Look up Matthew 5:21–24.

Is Jesus contradicting the Old Testament here, or is he pushing it to a radical conclusion?

5 The world of the Bible is very different from our own. In order to apply the message of the Bible to our own age we need to look very carefully at the principles involved.
For example, look up Romans 13:1–7.

Paul bases what he says on three timeless principles:
● *'The authorities that exist have been established by God' (v 1)*. God has put order, structure and authority into human society. These are essential elements if society is going to be just and peaceful.
● *'He is God's servant' (v 4)*. Those who have authority over others are expected to use it as God's representative. They should reflect his standards of right and wrong, of justice and of mercy.
● *'Give everyone what you owe him' (v 7)*. We all have responsibilities in return for privileges. Those in authority are responsible for our welfare; they should have our respect in return. We have the benefit of a well-ordered, well-run society; we must contribute to its upkeep in return.

These principles remain the same for all time, but what they meant in practical terms in the first century, and what they mean in a twentieth-century democracy might be very different.

THE 'PROBLEM' OF THE OLD TESTAMENT

The problem with the Old Testament is that it sometimes seems to be in conflict with the New Testament. God is seen to be backing the wars of his people in the Old Testament. In the New Testament, God's people are commanded to love their enemies, not wipe them out. Why do you suppose there is this difference? Does it reflect a change in the character of God, or a change in the identity of his people, or are there other reasons for the difference?

As we have already noted, we cannot just take two verses completely out of context – say, one from the Old Testament and one from the New – and then accuse them of saying opposite things. We have to take into account the overall purpose of the writer of the book in which they come, and ask what he is teaching about God, and why.

Down the centuries, people have got stuck on this problem of seeing major differences between the teaching of the Old Testament and the teaching of the New. How you decide to tackle the problem will depend largely on how you regard the Bible. Is it a collection of unreliable myths, showing how people's thinking about God has changed? Is it written in some sort of 'code' that has to be reinterpreted to be relevant for us today? Is it reliable teaching given to people by God, and the final authority on issues of right and wrong?

Some of the ways people deal with the differences

1 Abandon the Old Testament.
2 Spiritualize the Old Testament: change physical wars into spiritual battles.
3 See the teaching of the Old Testament as valid for believers who lived before Christ, but not for us who live after Christ and have his teaching on love and forgiveness.

4 See the Old Testament teaching as valid when it gives principles for behaviour, but not when it shows people in one particular culture working them out in practice. For example, the *general principle* in the Old Testament concerning marriage is that one man and one woman commit themselves exclusively to each other for life. But in practice, divorce was allowed, and polygamy was not condemned. In the New Testament, Jesus upholds the general principle as being God-given, but unmistakably regards divorce as originating in man's sinfulness (see Matthew 19:4–9).
5 See the whole of the Old Testament as valid for us – in that it gives general principles for behaviour, but accept that the New Testament pushes those principles to their logical (and radical) conclusions. 'Love your neighbour' is present in the Old Testament; Jesus pushes the definition of neighbour to its extreme in the parable of the Good Samaritan. Israelites were not just to regard other Jews as their neighbours, but were to see Gentiles as their neighbours too – even those Gentiles who were regarded as enemies.

Let's take an example and see what happens when we deal with it according to option 5.

● Look up Deuteronomy 5:20; 23:21–23 (Old Testament), and Matthew 5:33–37 (New Testament).
The Old Testament demands truthfulness but allows for oaths (vows). In the New Testament the demand is for a truthfulness that is so transparent that oaths and undertakings such as vows are no longer needed.

Think about it . . .

The Bible itself maintains that all of it is relevant and important (see 2 Timothy 3:16–17), so a solution needs to be found that takes seriously the message of the Old Testament. On this basis, only solutions 4 and 5 in the above list would be feasible.

This particular subject of war and pacifism brings people face to face with the problem of how to understand the Old Testament. Christians have to decide what their attitude is to the Old Testament before they start to think about this subject, as their attitude will affect what biblical evidence they use, and how they use it.

3
FACTS AND VALUES

3.1 THE FACTS OF LIFE

This section is all about facing the facts of life in a nuclear age.

ACTIVITY ONE

Alien

You will need to divide into pairs. One of you is an alien from outer space, the other is an ordinary person of the twentieth century.

The alien doesn't look any different from anybody else, being able to assume any shape, but he/she knows absolutely nothing about this planet earth. Write down some basic facts about this planet and how life is conducted on it, under the heading:

'WHAT EVERY ALIEN OUGHT TO KNOW.'

Make sure that you explain things very carefully to your aliens; remember they know *nothing* about earth. Choose the basic facts that will enable them to live here.

Share your basic facts with other members of the group.

Think about it . . .

This activity should help you to sort out what you think are the most important facts that someone should know about our planet. We all learn the facts of life about sex, but how many of us face the facts of life about war? How many people included the facts about violence and evil in their descriptions of life on this planet? How many included the facts about our arsenals of weapons that could destroy us, or the millions who have died under oppressive regimes?

We all live with a number of facts that enable us to relate to people, to work and to function within society. But our mind can't cope with some facts and it tends to react by pretending they're not there – as the poem below shows:

Dad

The trouble with me is
i take everything for granted
Cambodia – 50,000 dead gee whiz pass
    the salt.
i take wars for granted
My dad says its because i'm younger
    than the bomb
But the trouble with me is
i take the bomb for granted.
He says
i won't bloody well
take it for granted
when it drops on my head.

i take my head for granted.

(Brian McCabe)

Facts tend to have some effect on our behaviour. If I knew I would die tomorrow I would behave differently today. We cannot cope with very threatening facts for too long so our minds pretend they are not there. But every now and again these facts (such as the fact that we are not immortal) surface and change our priorities. There are certain facts about our armed and violent world that our minds can't face, and most of the time we ignore them because they are too threatening. That is part of our body's defence mechanism; we couldn't live perpetually terrified. But when we make decisions about our attitudes to war, we *must* make them in the light of the facts, no matter how frightening.

ACTIVITY TWO

Facts about our world

Below are some of the facts about war and pacifism. They include the beliefs and opinions of both pacifists and non-pacifists. Copy these on pieces of paper and put them in a hat. Pass the hat around and ask each person to take a piece of paper out of the hat and read it out.

FACTS

1 Military policy tends to assume that a rational and sane person is in charge of the 'button'. We cannot guarantee that; neither can we guarantee normal decision-making processes in the event of a nuclear strike. Communications would be devastated and decisions would be difficult to make in the ensuing chaos and panic.

2 There is an increased reliance on computers in decision-making. This could mean that time for human deliberation, discussion and reflection is reduced. No country yet relies totally on computers to take the decision to launch, but the technology to do this has been developed.

3 The medical services could not cope in the event of a nuclear strike. Most of the big hospitals are situated in towns and cities, the very targets of nuclear weapons. The medical services have already warned the government that they could not cope with the volume of casualties in the event of such a strike. The comparatively small bomb that hit Hiroshima killed 270 of the city's 298 doctors.

4 Fires would break out in the wake of any nuclear explosion but most of the equipment and personnel needed to fight them would have already been wiped out.

5 Treating burns victims is a specialized area of medicine. Even if the medical facilities were unaffected they would be unable to cope.

6 If a city like London were hit with four nuclear warheads, it is estimated that 76% of the population would be lost – approximately five million people.

7 After a nuclear hit, sanitation would become a major problem. Raw sewage would mix with the water supply and people would face mass epidemics.

8 Many people would die immediately from the effects of blast and radiation. Others would die slowly over the following months and years as a result of fall-out that is carried in the air. Diseases such as cancer are the long-term results of such radiation. Cancer deaths in the millions could be expected after a nuclear strike.

9 The genetic effects of mass radiation are incalculable. Abortions and abnormalities could be expected for many generations.

10 Survivors of a nuclear attack would find it difficult to satisfy even the most basic human needs. Food, fuel, housing and clothing would all be in short supply.

11 The effect on the economy of a major nuclear strike would be devastating. Many factories and machines would have been destroyed, along with the banking system.

12 Some scientists believe that an all-out nuclear war could change the climate, either raising or lowering the average temperatures. This means there would be either increased radiation or a nuclear winter.

13 If everyone in the world was given adequate food, water, education, health and housing it would cost approximately £9,000,000,000. That is as much as the world spends every two weeks on arms. (From calculations in the *New Internationalist* based on figures produced by the World Bank 1980, quoted in *The Nuclear Age* by CEM, published in 1982.)

14 Nuclear weapons are proliferating; more countries are acquiring them. Not all of these countries are stable politically.

15 Smaller nuclear weapons are now being made. They are more accurate and less deadly. Unfortunately they are designed for tactical fighting rather than deterrence. That is a dangerous shift in policy. Once the nuclear barrier has been crossed, what is to stop it escalating? Even the use of small, battlefield nuclear weapons would cause great destruction as any such war is likely to be fought in densely-populated central Europe.

16 500,000 scientists work on weapons research – one quarter of all research scientists.

17 Food production would be drastically reduced. The destruction of farm equipment, land and transport systems – plus the problems of contamination – mean that food could be in short supply.

18 The world has far more weapons than it needs even for deterrence; we can kill each other many times over.

19 Computers sometimes make mistakes. Between 1979 and 1980 there were a number of military computer failures. For 3–6 minutes the USA thought that the USSR had launched an attack. There were 147 false alarms in eighteen months.

20 There has been peace in Europe for forty years. Many feel such a peace would not have existed without the atomic bomb.

21 There have been 127 wars in other parts of the globe since the Second World War. Wars are now fought outside the European theatre.

22 More people die in peace time than in war. Many people live in conditions and under regimes that we in the West would consider intolerable. It has been estimated that more people have died in Vietnam since the Americans left than during the war. In Cambodia one third to one half of the population has been killed in mass genocide. Is war always the worst thing that could happen?

23 Six million Jews were killed under Hitler. The total would have been higher if the Allies had not fought to resist him.

24 Money spent on arms could be spent on other things such as the education and health services, but if a country is invaded there will be no education or health service to protect.

25 Disarmament was tried once before, prior to the rise of Hitler. It left England dangerously unprepared.

26 The Warsaw Pact is vastly superior

in its number of tanks. These can only be met effectively by nuclear weapons.

27 Nuclear weapons are a last resort; they are to stop war. Their use is not envisaged and they have not been used (other than in tests) since the initial drops on Hiroshima and Nagasaki.

28 Use of conventional weapons does not always lead to full-scale war. There have been many conventional wars since 1945 but none of them has escalated into nuclear war.

29 The peace movement plays into the hands of the Soviet Union. Any real peace movement behind the 'Iron Curtain' is suppressed.

30 Life without defence is unimaginable. As long as people are not perfect, defence – either conventional or nuclear – will be necessary.

31 Biological weapons have long-term effects, but we do not yet know what these are. During the last war the Scottish island of Gruinard was infected with anthrax and it will be contaminated for hundreds of years.

32 Chemical weapons were used in Vietnam and had serious genetic and environmental consequences; it is not only nuclear weapons that are terrifying in their effects.

33 There is evidence that we have the technology to create defensive weapons that could make many of our present offensive weapons look obsolete. These are not fully developed yet but might provide a 'safer' alternative to some of our present systems.

34 Nuclear weapons have done some good in that they have made people face up to the horrors of all war, and they have stripped war of any false glory.

35 The weapons that threaten life may be the very things that preserve it. Nuclear weapons may have produced such a 'balance of terror' that no one will use them. Even the use of conventional weapons is now restricted between the superpowers. Removing nuclear weapons would make life unstable again.

36 It is easy to criticize governments and spell out the horrors of war but someone has to make decisions, and until alternative weapons are developed we have to live with the results of past inventions (present weapons).

37 We have to face the fact that some of the freedoms we now enjoy are the result of wars. If we lived under an oppressive regime where basic human rights were denied us, we would not be so quick to condemn violence.

Think about it . . .

Facts on their own can be frightening, whether they are about a world inadequately defended, or about the defences we have. However unpleasant these facts are, they need to be faced when coming to a decision. The pacifist can't ignore the reality of evil, and those who favour nuclear deterrence need to face up to the nature of those weapons.

CHECK OUT THE BIBLE

The Bible is always realistic; it doesn't pretend about war and evil.

● Read Habakkuk 1:2–4; 3:16–19
Habakkuk watched the destruction of his nation through war. Many of his people died in battle or from famine and disease. Many more were taken off to Babylon as slaves.

How did Habakkuk feel about what was happening around him? How did he cope with it? ▶▶

▶▶
The Bible is realistic about the horrors of war, but in the face of those horrors calls for trust in God as well as adequate preparation. Weapons on their own were never enough.

● Read Isaiah 7:1–9
What was Judah called to do here in the face of an invasion?

● Read Judges 6:12–16
On some occasions Israel and Judah were called by God to fight. Here Gideon is called on to rescue the Israelites from the oppression of the Midianites.

● Read Amos 1:3–15 and Isaiah 65:17–25
Although God did command his people to go to war with certain nations, he warned of harsh judgment for those who were ruthless and took a perverse delight in war. Throughout the Bible, the idea of global peace and harmony is upheld as being God's ultimate goal.

Think about it . . .

This session looks very depressing, but you cannot weigh up the possible alternatives unless you have first faced a few of the facts.

One thing is essential in this study: although we need to focus on the size of the problem, we also need to re-focus on the greatness of God. He is *in control* of world history, and he is also concerned to help us think through the part we have to play in it.

● Read together Isaiah 40:10–17, 28–31; 41:1–7, or close your eyes while it is read to you.
What pictures come to your mind while this is being read? Share them with the rest of the group.

However depressing this subject may look, the Bible maintains a confident hope in God. It paints a picture of God as caring and involved, even in the most frightening situations.

3.2 THE NUCLEAR UMBRELLA

When deciding about the issues of war and pacifism it is necessary to stop and think very carefully about values. If a Christian is not a pacifist, he might decide he should be actively involved in war by fighting, in order to defend certain values. What might such a person consider to be so valuable that he would go to war to protect? What might he consider so evil that he would believe it worth going to war to prevent? Some Christians are pacifists and would never actually fight to defend values they believe in, though they would use every other means, including giving up their own life if necessary. What would they consider worth dying for, or worth dying to prevent?

ACTIVITY ONE

Transformation

Think your way through your normal day. (Where do you go? What do you do? Who are your friends? What is your family like?) Then imagine you are all of the following:

a. Staggeringly handsome/beautiful
b. Highly intelligent
c. Athletic
d. Heir/heiress to a fortune
e. The son/daughter of extremely rich and powerful parents.

Think through your day again, imagining you have changed as above. How would life be different?

Think about it . . .

Few of us fit the above description! But we can imagine how life might be different if we did. Did you find yourself thinking like a 'spoilt child' in the activity above? Those who are rich and powerful don't often have to work hard at making friends – people tend to be friendly towards them for all the wrong reasons. Other people might do as someone says because of who her parents are, rather than out of respect for the person herself.

Since the Second World War the West has relied heavily on nuclear weapons. They are comparatively cheap and have proved effective in maintaining peace. Alexander Solzhenitsyn has described the result as life under the 'nuclear umbrella'. With the bomb in the background there has been no war between the superpowers. The bomb has produced a form of pacifism, because nations are reluctant to confront each other for fear of nuclear weapons being used. This has meant that sometimes injustice has gone unchecked for fear of starting a war.

The West has grown wealthy and powerful; maybe we have behaved like the 'spoilt child' in the first activity, caring more about living standards than about justice and love.

ACTIVITY TWO

The values washing line

You will need a length of string or a washing line that will stretch the length of the room. The line should be tied to chairs at opposite ends of the room. You will also need pens, paper and some pegs.

VALUES LIST

Life
Freedom
Security
Justice
Freedom from poverty for your own
. country
Freedom from poverty for other
    countries
Freedom from oppression for your own
    country
Freedom from oppression for other .
    countries
National pride
Getting more land
Self-defence
A particular way of life
Religious freedom
Peace
Wealth
Defending a neighbour
Spreading your nation's influence

Keeping/getting a particular political
system

Write each of the above values on a piece
of paper and give one to each member of
the group. Fix a label to one end of the
string, reading 'Top priority', and
another to the other end reading 'Lowest
priority'. Ask the group one by one to
affix their 'value' to the line in the place
of priority they would give it. They can
move other people's values if necessary.
Use the pegs to secure them.

Think about it . . .

It is not easy to put things in order. Every
time we give one thing priority,
something else has to go further down the
line. Ideally, most of us would like to
have everything as a priority, but in life
choices have to be made which are never
easy.

CHECK OUT THE BIBLE

(Divide the group into smaller groups and
give each group one or two sections to
discuss. If further guidance is needed,
refer to the comments below the
references.)

The Bible has a lot to say about values.
Look up the verses listed below and
discuss the values they put across. Would
you agree with them? Do you think they

are still legitimate values for today? Say
why, or why not.

● Read Genesis 9:5–6 and Deuteronomy
19:11–13
Life was valuable in the Bible. The
existence of the death penalty does not
deny the value of human life but
underlines it. To take a life was so bad
that the murderer's life was forfeited. ▶▶

▶▶

• Read Deuteronomy 13:12–18.
The enormity and frequency of judgments on idolatry in the Bible show that holiness, truth and goodness were valued very highly – sometimes more highly than life itself. It was the *type* of life that mattered. How do Jesus' words in Mark 8:34–36 relate to this?

• Read Proverbs 14:31; 19:17 and Amos 2:6–7
The poor and powerless come under God's special care. A society is judged by its treatment of them.

• Read James 5:1–6
The Bible is very outspoken against those who make themselves wealthy at the expense of others.

• Read Psalm 72:1–4, 12–14
Justice should be brought about and maintained by government; but ordinary people also have a responsibility to see that justice is done.

• Read Micah 6:8 and James 2:14–17
Religion must result in practical goodness. Without practical love and care for others, 'religiosity' is useless and worthless.

• Read Matthew 5:9 and Romans 8:20–21
Christians are called to work for peace at all levels of life. They want to see the whole universe working again in harmony, because that is the goal of God their Father. 'Like father, like son!'

• Read Judges 7:1–7
There is no doubt that God sanctioned certain wars in the Old Testament. But the wars he sanctioned were always *very clearly* commanded by God. The victory was regarded as a victory for *him* (for truth, righteousness and justice), rather than for the 'winning' nation; and the trust of the side who fought for God was in him, rather than in the weapons they used.

The Bible clearly gives a high priority to values such as justice, peace and love. They are at the very heart of its teaching about God. In an ideal world, values such as justice and peace would not be in conflict; but we live is a world marred by evil and where people's understanding of values differs. Love and justice might, for example, point people towards looking after their neighbour, but if that neighbour is being attacked by another person, peace may have to be sacrificed in order to love the victim and show justice to the attacker.

According to the Bible, people are valuable because of who made them. Even the worst person is to be treated with the dignity of someone made in the image of God, even if that image is marred.

Think about it . . .

Think about this yourself. What would you decide is worth dying for? What is worth fighting for? Is there anything you think is so evil that it would be worth going to war to prevent it, or do you consider war itself to be the greatest evil?

4
PEACE AND WAR

4.1 WHAT IS PEACE?

Peace is a much misunderstood word. In this section we are going to look at the biblical understanding of peace.

ACTIVITY ONE

Word association test

Put two large sheets of paper on the wall. Label one 'Peace' and the other 'War'. If there isn't enough room for this, give each member of the group a piece of paper with the two titles on. Everybody has one minute to write down as many things as they can, associated with war and peace.

Look at the two lists. Are they lists of opposites or are there any common factors? Is there any overlap? Keep these lists as you will need them later.

Think about it . . .

People tend to think of peace in negative terms – peace is when the fighting stops. But that is not how the Bible refers to peace. Peace in the Bible is about right relationships. It is health and wholeness, order and contentment. It is linked to prosperity and is closely tied to justice. God is shown to be actively involved in our world, affecting the course of history and working at every level for peace and harmony. It is through Jesus that God

brings true peace to the world, by bringing people into a right relationship with himself. That relationship is then reflected by those who have taken his peace into their own lives, bringing healing and reconciliation to others. Christians believe that the peace of a right relationship with God, through Jesus Christ, is the *only* deep and lasting peace. Of course, the political peace that Christians may know in world events, day by day, is a very fragile affair. Ultimately the world will not be peaceful until Jesus comes again.

ACTIVITY TWO

Peace is . . .

You will need paper and felt-tipped pens. You have probably seen the 'Love is . . .' cartoons. Choose two or three of the references below and draw a 'Peace is . . .' cartoon for each, illustrating the aspect of peace it expresses.

BIBLICAL REFERENCES TO PEACE

● Isaiah 2:4

Christians believe that there will be a time when God will intervene to end all evil and war. That is difficult to picture! Try to imagine the 9 o'clock news without any references to violence or wrong.

● Psalm 4:8

Peace can mean security. But it is more

than a 'Linus blanket', it is the *knowledge* that God loves you and is always with you.

● Genesis 15:15
Peace comes when the struggle of life stops.

● Isaiah 48:18 and Romans 5:1
Peace starts with obedience to God; a person in that relationship with God will affect others around him or her.

● Isaiah 53:5 and Colossians 1:20
Peace costs.

● 1 Corinthians 14:33
Peace is the sign that God is at work.

● Luke 2:14
Peace became a practical possibility for all mankind when the prince of peace was born into our world.

● Matthew 5:9 and 2 Corinthians 5:18–20
Christians are called to be peacemakers.

● Mark 9:50
Peace is between individual people as well as governments and nations.

● Ephesians 2:14–17
Peace breaks down prejudice.

● Philippians 4:7
Peace is beyond our understanding; it is not something we can create by ourselves.

● John 14:27
Nothing can shatter the peace that God gives.

● Romans 12:18
Peaceful people avoid the wrong sort of conflict.

● Ephesians 6:15
The gospel is the good news of peace in a world torn by conflict.

● Psalm 72:1–7
This is a description of a truly peaceful kingdom.

Make a display of all the cartoons.

Think about it . . .

There is no cheap peace in the Bible. Peace costs. Peace doesn't paper over the cracks; it is evidence of a change at a deep level. Making peace does not mean keeping quiet; sometimes people have to 'rock the boat' in order to make peace.

For example, a nation can be peaceful – in the sense that there is no war going on – under a tyrannical regime. But if the people are treated unjustly and without dignity, that would not be peaceful in the Bible's terms. It would only be peaceful when people had changed that situation. Initially this might involve them in protest and challenging the state. The recent overthrow of President Marcos in the Philippines involved protest and disobedience to the state. But that protest and subsequent change of government eventually led to a more peaceful situation, in biblical terms, than continuing under a corrupt regime after change had become a possibility.

A peaceful world is a united and just world. Peace is not merely the absence of armed conflict; it is the absence of disorder at all levels. Peace in this world, however, is sometimes established *through* conflict. If people think of peace only as the absence of war, then many evils go unchallenged. Millions die in 'peace time'. In the Luwero Triangle in Uganda the piles of skulls and bones in many villages are evidence of the massacres that can take place in a country not at war.

Think about it . . .

Think carefully about who the peacemakers are. Is it only pacifists who make peace or can people in the armed forces also act as peacemakers?

4.2 WHY DOES WAR HAPPEN?

This question is asked in the Bible, and a very direct answer is given: wars happen because of greed and selfishness in the human heart. This is the root *cause* of all war because it breeds injustice of all sorts. But there are many *motives* which a nation might have for going to war, other than the directly selfish motive of getting more for itself at the expense of others. In this section we will be looking at some of these motives and will try to decide which, if any, can acceptably lead a Christian into war.

1 PREJUDICE

ACTIVITY ONE

Each person will need a small piece of paper or card with three vertical lines on it. The three lines indicate three lives. Sit in a circle with some friends, facing outwards so that you cannot see each other. The first person in the group makes a statement such as: 'I can't stand people with curly hair'. The next person does the same but chooses a different characteristic. Each time a statement is made people cross off one of their 'lives' if the statement is relevant to them. When everybody in the circle has made a statement, check the cards to see how many people are 'dead'. How many people survived your prejudices?

Some of these prejudices may look very superficial, but prejudice always is. A person is prejudiced if he or she 'pre-judges' a situation or person – making up his or her mind about them before taking any of the facts into account. Prejudice is based on misunderstanding and ignorance. Many wars have been caused by prejudice and ignorance. People are often afraid of things they do not know or are unfamiliar with, and this ignorance may be exploited by the government planning on war.

People of the 'enemy' nation may be caricatured, and the differences emphasized, in order to increase dislike of them.

The problem of prejudice has to be dealt with by each of us. If it is dealt with within people it is difficult to start a war based on it! In the Bible, difference and variety are seen as gifts of God. In aspects that really matter, all people are seen as being the same. Look up the following verses:

- Galatians 3:28
Differences are not to be ignored, but people are to be treated equally.

- Acts 10:34–35, Exodus 23:2–9
God makes it plain that *he* doesn't have 'favourites', and so doesn't expect us to either! We should treat all people with respect and not be influenced by how rich they are, what social 'class' they come from, or what nationality they happen to be.

2 ENVY

ACTIVITY TWO

Get into pairs. One person in each pair needs to take a small object (such as a ring or a shoe) and put it on their lap. The other person has one minute to use any method they like to try to get the object. Stop at the end of one minute and share with the rest of the group the different methods used to acquire the object.

- How often did bargaining work?
- How many people used force?
- How many tried blackmail?
- Were other methods used?

Greed lies behind a great many wars. It is often an attempt to acquire land or resources. The Bible has some strong statements on greed; look up the following:

- Luke 12:15
What do you think Jesus meant? How does our society assess people's value?

- 1 Corinthians 10:23–24
How does greed turn people in on themselves?

- Philippians 4:11–12
What does contentment depend on?

- James 4:1–3
The Bible doesn't mince its words on greed, but how can envy lead to war?

Can Christians ever support a war that is based on greed and envy?

3 NATIONAL HONOUR AND PRIDE

ACTIVITY THREE

Think about the sort of things people boast about. What makes you look big in front of your friends? What makes you look stupid? Make two lists: one of things that make people look stupid, one of things that impress others.

Nations go in for boasting as much as individuals do, and when their pride is hurt they sometimes retaliate with war.
    The Bible states that a nation should be proud of things such as justice and love. Psalm 72 describes a nation's true glory. In this Psalm prosperity is linked to the king's goodness, but although riches and land are often seen as a blessing in the Bible, they are never a basis for boasting. A rich and powerful nation without compassion is poverty-stricken in God's view.

Look up:
- Revelation 2:9; 3:17
How would you describe your own nation: rich, in the biblical sense, or poor?

Christians have to think carefully about any war fought on the basis of national pride. If it is only a matter of hurt egos is there really a basis for going to war?

ACTIVITY FOUR

The following activities are based on encounters between individuals. We are using situations such as mugging and burglary to help us decide what is reasonable on an international scale, although clearly there are many differences which have to be taken into account.

Imagine you are walking along a road. Someone threatens you with physical violence. How do you respond? Choose your most likely response out of the following:

a. Fight
b. Try to talk them out of it
c. Try to defend yourself without, as far as possible, hurting them.
d. Carry a personal alarm/scream
e. Threaten them with the weapon you carry for such occasions
f. Take evasive action
g. Do nothing

If you have room to set up this situation and role-play your responses, do so. One member of the group will need to be the mugger who demands your money. Choose another to be the victim, and work out the different methods of approaching the situation, using drama.

Think about it . . .

Mugging sometimes happens on an international scale. As we have seen, there are differences between individuals and the state, but there are also principles common to both that can be drawn out:

1 The individual has a right to exist, as a person created by God.
2 The state as a collection of individuals therefore has a right to exist.
3 In order to stay in existence, the state, as a body invested with authority by God and responsible for its citizens, has a right to defend itself when threatened. See Romans 13:1–7; 1 Peter 2:13–17.

This does not mean that the state can fight *any* war. But it does mean that it can fight when threatened, and the majority of Christians feel that they could co-operate in such a war.

To apply these texts to war, we have to extend the state's 'policing' role (the right to maintain law and order within its own boundaries) to the international field. This may be perfectly valid, but it must not be done automatically and without due consideration. The pacifist does not deny the state's right to exist, but would say that this right (and hence the right to self-defence) can be forfeited.

The pacifist would take Matthew 5:39–40 literally, whereas some would treat it as hyperbole (exaggeration to make a point). Many pacifists who take this literally would say that it doesn't just apply to private ethics, but to international ethics too. Others believe that these verses, and the rest of the Sermon on the Mount, were meant for personal morality and cannot be applied to international affairs.

Many Christian pacifists maintain that

a state can defend itself, using arms if necessary, but deny the Christian's right to participate, except in non-violent ways. The thinking behind this is that it is one thing for *Christians* to use non-violent means of resistance, but they cannot call a nation of largely non-Christians to national martyrdom by forfeiting its right to take arms to defend itself. Some pacifists recognize this and, instead of trying to influence national policy and make the state live according to Christian morality, they aim to witness to the state by living a personally non-violent lifestyle.

ACTIVITY FIVE

Repeat the scene as for activity four, but this time there are two people walking along and the mugger threatens one of them. What do you do when your friend is threatened? Go through the list of options again. Does it make any difference to how you respond that it is someone else who is threatened?

Jesus said that, next to loving God, the most important command was to love one's neighbour (see Luke 10:27). The trouble is that we have more than one neighbour; who do we show love to, the mugger or the friend? To a large extent, our answer will depend on what we mean by 'love'. Is it loving to allow the mugger to go on hurting others?

Love is not the only command to take into account in our decision, though it is the command by which the others are interpreted. God also demands justice (see Micah 6:8). Is it just to let evil go unchecked? Pacifists do not necessarily leave evil unchecked, they fight it by different, non-violent means, often at great personal cost. In this case, the pacifist's response might be to take the victim's place.

It is difficult for a pacifist to defend members of another country. Pacifists point out that there are diplomatic, political and economic channels that can be used instead of recourse to war. All Christians would want these channels to be used first, with war as a last resort. Christians who are not pacifists often feel that they can participate on humanitarian grounds in wars that are in defence of others.

Think about it . . .
We have only looked at a few of the motives for war, but it should be clear that Christians will take into account a wide range of biblical teaching when they are deciding whether a particular war is legitimate or not, and what role they should play in it.

5
POWER

5.1 POWER, AUTHORITY, FORCE AND VIOLENCE

In this chapter we are going to take a brief look at the basic concepts of power, authority, force and violence. The definitions which follow are extremely brief and simple. Expand on them if you wish.

● **Power** is the ability to put intentions into action. It can be used legitimately or illegitimately; it can be used for good or ill.

● **Force** is one means of exercising power and authority.

● **Authority** is the right to exercise power. All power and authority derive ultimately from God. God delegates some authority to humanity, for example to parents and the state. Jesus, in his reply to Pilate in John 19:11, recognized that all authority came from God.

● **Violence** is the immoral use of force. This may sound clear in theory, but is sometimes difficult to distinguish the two in practice. One person's force is another's violence. Force can describe anything from smacking a child, to war. The law relies on force: without force to back it up it has no 'bite'. The term 'force' may be used to cover a whole spectrum of activities, so that 'restraining a criminal' is part of the same spectrum as 'dropping a bomb'. But common sense tells us we have moved so far along the spectrum that we really need to use another term to describe the action of dropping a bomb, such as 'lethal force'.

When pacifists object to the use of force in war, they are not necessarily condemning all use of force. Some pacifists support the use of force by the police, and other types of coercion; it is only 'lethal force' they object to. Violence, by the above definition, is not a Christian option.

It is important to recognize that whether the use of force is legitimate or not depends on *how* it is used, not on *who* wields it. The state can use force immorally, as in the case of Germany under Hitler, or the Ugandan government under Idi Amin. The tyrannical use of power can (and should) be resisted legitimately by those who are not in a position of power or authority, because the state loses its authority once it, as God's representative, acts in a way that is out of keeping with his character. Pacifists and those who support the use of force differ over the means used to resist the state, but agree that the state should be resisted when it becomes evil or demands a degree of allegiance, obedience or worship that people should only give to God. Most Christians would see the use of force as the last measure, not the first – to be employed when all else has failed.

ACTIVITY ONE

Force scale

You will need an old roll of wallpaper and some felt-tipped pens. Draw a long line on the roll of paper. Mark various points along the line and label them, starting at one end of the line with a mild use of force, such as 'restraining a child to stop her hurting herself' and ending with an example of 'lethal force', such as 'declaring war'.

Between these two marks fill in different degrees of force and write down who you think has the authority to wield them.

● *For example*: 'Restraining a criminal' – 'a policeman'.

In each of these cases, discuss how force can become violence.

● *For example*: A degree of force can be used to discipline a child. This is rightfully exercised by the parents. It becomes violence when too much force is used, it is then 'child abuse'.

Think about it . . .

Force itself is not wrong, though pacifists would say that the use of 'lethal force' is. Force becomes wrong for all Christians when it is used immorally, and it must be resisted whoever wields it. God may give authority to the state to use the sword to punish evil, but that is not a blank cheque. Christians need to be selective in their use of force. Paul's words in Romans 13:1–7, and 1 Peter 2:13–17, cannot be used automatically as a justification for war. They are primarily about internal policing. The state is given the power to punish the guilty and protect the innocent. Force can be used in this context, as the word 'sword' indicates.

These verses raise two major issues:
1 Should the pursuit of justice stop at a national boundary?
2 Modern weapons do not necessarily punish the guilty and leave the innocent untouched. Modern warfare affects everyone, particularly if nuclear weapons are used.

A Christian response to tyranny or unprovoked aggression may well be a selective use of force. But Christians have to think carefully about the means used, and no one nation can act as 'policeman' for others, or see itself as a world crusader. The means we now have at our disposal make a nonsense of such an attitude, which is now a highly dangerous one to hold.

ACTIVITY TWO

(This activity can be omitted if time is short.)

Under the influence

Ask a member of the group to lie down on a large sheet of paper, with their feet together, so that you can draw around them. When you have done this, draw arrows around the 'person', directed towards them, showing who or what has power over them. Label each arrow with the name of the person or thing that wields the power.

Think through your own life and decide who has power over you. Power can come in many forms:

- influence (the power of example)
- emotional power (our emotional needs that give others power over us)
- moral power (the power of feeling – or being told – we *ought* to do certain things)
- physical power (the power other people have to *make* us do certain things)
- legal power (the power the law has to make us do certain things)
- internal power (the drives and needs that our body dictates and which have power over us, such as hunger or our sex drive. There are also powerful drives that are a result of our personality, such as ambition and fear).

Think carefully about the power other people have over you. How much do you decide to do because you *want* to? How much do you *have* to do? How could each of the powers above be misused? How would you suffer as a result?

Think about it . . .

As you probably noticed from the activity, we are all on the receiving end of other people's power, but everybody also exercises some sort of power over others. Think about the power you exercise: the influence that you have, the needs in others that you fulfil, so giving you power over them. It is not only force that needs

exercising with care. All power needs to be used creatively and not destructively.

CHECK OUT THE BIBLE

Look up the following passages and sort them into two groups, according to the way in which power is exercised.

- Philippians 2:5–11
- Genesis 1:1–3
- Genesis 6:5–8
- 2 Corinthians 12:9
- Joshua 6:1–5
- Ephesians 1:19–20
- Judges 7:1–7
- Deuteronomy 7:7
- Mark 9:6
- 1 Samuel 17:41–46
- Matthew 24:30
- Matthew 8:23–27

What two different expressions of power do your two groups reveal?

Think about it . . .

Power can be expressed in different ways. God used his power to create the earth, and to flood it. God's power working through Jesus raised the dead, healed the sick and rebuked the storm.

At other times, God's power is expressed through human weakness. Gideon's army was small; David was the youngest son in his family but defeated Goliath; God came to earth as a helpless baby; and the symbol of victory and power for the Christian is a cross.

Christians exercise both types of power. Some wield authority; some have force at their command; some exercise enormous influence; and some have legal powers. Others exercise God's power through apparent weakness. Mother

Teresa is not wealthy, she holds no political power, but her life has had an enormous influence on others. Martin Luther King commanded no army but exercised enormous political power through his influence.

There is power in weakness *when that weakness is handed over to God*. It is one of the Bible's central messages, and the experience of many Christians, that when they admit their own weakness and ask for God's strength, God's power becomes evident in them. Paul summed this up when he said, 'When I am weak, then I am strong' (2 Corinthians 12:10). He describes power in weakness in detail in 2 Corinthians 4:7–12.

For the pacifist the concept of power in weakness means that he or she will not use force as a means of resisting aggression. Non-pacifists accept the other view of power – power in strength. Nations were armed in both the Old and New Testaments. Whatever view of power you take, whether you are a pacifist or not, the biblical principle is the same: it is God's power that is to be relied on (Psalm 33:16–19).

Pacifists believe that God sometimes acts directly to save. Non-pacifists use weapons to fight, but they are to put their trust in God, not just the weapons. The Old Testament (hardly a pacifist's book) *condemns* a sole trust in weapons and soldiers (see Isaiah 31:1–3). The Babylonians are a picture of the wrong attitude to power. They are described in Habakkuk 1:11 as 'Guilty men whose own strength is their god'.

5.2 TAMING THE TIGER

During this unit we will be looking at technology, and at what control we can exercise over military technology.

ACTIVITY ONE

(The following account should be read to the group with considerable expression – but not with total seriousness!)

The pilot is dead
Imagine that you are on Concorde for the first time. The air hostess looks a bit worried but when you ask her what is wrong she says that everything is fine and there's nothing to worry about. After a while you notice that there is a lot of frantic activity going on and the plane begins to lunge about. A worried-looking steward emerges and asks if there is anyone on board who can fly a plane. You have had three lessons in a light aircraft but have never flown 'solo'. Nobody else is admitting to any flying experience so you volunteer. The steward takes you forward to the cockpit and you stare in amazement at the terrifying array of instruments. This is nothing like your light aircraft. You look around the cockpit. The pilot is slumped on one side, dead from a heart attack. The co-pilot is writhing in agony with food poisoning and

the auto pilot has broken down. You are faced with a choice: learn rather quickly how to fly this plane or leave this immensely complicated piece of machinery out of control with the possibility of tremendous loss of life.

Think up an ending for this disaster story. How are you going to land this plane? Does it land safely? If you want to, work out a small sketch to illustrate your ending.

Think about it . . .

A plane like Concorde is an enormously complicated piece of machinery. Normally it is under the control of the pilot. In an emergency it can be put under the guidance of the control tower, with control exercised through another person.

Our society looks rather like a plane that is out of control: now that people do not generally recognize God's authority, who is going to decide where our technology is to take us? We are leap-frogging from one invention to the next with no real thought being given to the purpose or the consequences. We need to look at this seriously, particularly within the field of military technology. We need to think very carefully about whose control it is under and in what direction it is going.

A PARABLE

In India a parable is told about four brothers. Each brother went off to learn a skill. After many years the brothers met up again and demonstrated their skills to each other. The first brother said he had learnt to put flesh onto bones. So he picked up a bone from the jungle floor and clothed it with flesh, not knowing it was the bone of a lion. The next brother had learnt how to add hide and hair to the flesh, which he did. The third brother added matching limbs and the fourth brother gave it life. The lion stretched its new limbs, shook its mane, turned round and ate the brothers.

OUR MILITARY TECHNOLOGY

Are we creating a 'lion' with our technology that may turn round and eat us? The same technology can be used for many different purposes. A weapon that can be used offensively can also be used defensively. The American 'Star Wars' programme is an attempt to develop a system whose primary purpose is defence. John St John, in his book *Religion and Social Justice* (RMEP, 1985) speculates on the possible effects of this shift of emphasis, and introduces the hypothesis that even conventional weapons could become redundant:

'A more positive approach [than trying to match weapon for weapon] may come from the considerable technical improvements in conventional defensive weapons. Some experts now believe these to be sufficiently efficient to permit the West to dispense with battlefield nuclear shields. The basis of this new defensive posture would be an independent bloc of western European powers in alliance with the USA. As Stan Windass, co-director of Just Defence, explains:

". . . There is an accumulating mass of evidence to suggest that, if you really get your defence objectives clear, the means of stopping an invasion by tanks, ships and aircraft are becoming increasingly economical. The cost of destroying a tank effectively, even in adverse weather and in battlefield conditions, is one per cent of the price of a tank. It could well be that tanks, ships and aircraft as a means of invasion are becoming as obsolete as dinosaurs in the light of advancing technology." '

Technology can be used to make the world a safer place. The defensive weapons as described above would not solve all our problems concerning nuclear weapons, but might lead to a reduction in their numbers and in the likelihood of their being used.

Think about it . . .

At the moment the tail is wagging the dog – new weapons are invented and policies have to be formulated to deal with them.

Technology needs direction and control. It is not a 'god' to be obeyed without question. It needs above all Christian values, creative wisdom and a recognition that God is the true owner of this world; we are only tenants responsible for looking after it.

CHECK OUT THE BIBLE

1 God is the ultimate creator of the world. This doesn't just mean that he made it in the first place but that minute by minute he is sustaining it, keeping it going, continuing to give life to the people and creatures in it (see Hebrews 1:3). This world is entrusted to humanity to look after in partnership with God. We are responsible for the welfare of the world; it is not just a quarry of materials to be used up as we like.

How does this come out in the following passages?
- Genesis chapter 1
- Psalm 50:9–12
- Psalm 100:1–3

▶▶

- Psalm 8:1–9
- Leviticus 25:23

What is humanity required to do with this world? How would recognizing God as the creator and owner of the world change the way people live in it? Technology (military or civil) can enable people to either look after the world or destroy it. We have to decide which uses of our technology are helpful, and which are destructive.

2 'Wisdom' in the Bible is not the same as 'intelligence'. It is the ability to make the right use of knowledge. Wisdom recognizes the interdependence of everything: everything depends on something else. If we pollute the sea, for instance, there will be a chain reaction across a wide section of wildlife. Look up Proverbs 3:13–20. Wisdom works with creation, not against it. Why do you think the writer valued wisdom so highly? Which does our society value the most – wisdom, or intelligence?

3 The Bible acknowledges that God is the one in control of the world.

- Look up Isaiah 40:21–24
  How can God be regarded as in control when we hear on the news of so much that is going wrong in the world? The Bible makes it quite clear that God *is* in control but it also asserts that God gave humanity the freedom to choose good or evil, hence the evil we hear about on the news. The Bible also asserts that the power of evil was defeated once and for all on the cross and so it is certain that good will eventually triumph. History is not aimless; God is intimately involved with his creation and he will one day bring evil to a visible and decisive end.

4 It is only people, and not machines, who can make moral choices and who will one day answer for them. We must not let machines take away our power to make those decisions.

- Look up the following verses:
  1 Kings 18:21
  Matthew 25:31–46
  What decisions were these people asked to make? How can technology and machines be used to take away the ability of people to make such choices?

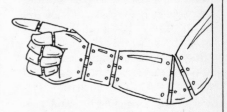

5 As we have seen, the Bible says that people are made 'in the image of God'. There have been many discussions over exactly what this means, but part at least of the meaning is that people are able to relate to each other and to God. This is one of the most fundamental aspects of being human. It is therefore very important to protect this ability. We need to look at our technology, both military and civil, and ask if it aids relationships or hinders them. Machines can free people from boring tasks, but they can also replace or prevent relationships.

- Look up Genesis 1:26
  What does this say about people's relationship to God and to each other? Think of ways in which technology can help relationships. Think of ways in which it hinders personal relationships. This may not look relevant to our topic of war, but military technology is only the

▶▶

▶▶

application of our technological skills to the realm of war. If we think we need to control the use of those skills in military life, then we need to think, too, about their control in civilian life.

6 The Bible speaks of life as being a gift from God. By that it means not just survival, but life in all its fullness.

- Read John 10:10
  God's original ideal was that people should live full and constructive lives as they worked 'alongside' him in the world. Jesus came to restore that 'working relationship' and everything else that went with it. How can our technology add to the quality of life? How can our technology make the quality of life poorer?

War was allowed – even commanded – in the Bible, but within certain limits. The environment was protected and so was the next generation (see Deuteronomy 20). Life was to continue after war.

Think about it . . .

Technology is not, in itself, evil; neither is it outside the realm of morality. We must decide where we are going to allow technology to take us. Most of us feel daunted by technology, and maybe insignificant in the face of it. But we are the ones who create the demands which are met by technology.

Take an example: conventional weapons, which are less destructive than nuclear, are more costly. Would we be prepared to pay more for a 'safer' system of weapons? Nuclear weapons have been considered a cheap option. Research into 'defensive' weapons (which could be used as part of a non-nuclear, non-provocative defence strategy) would also be expensive – though once the research stage was past they would be cheaper. For the Christian it is a matter of 'putting our money where our mouth is'. Would people pay extra taxes so that there could be research into different, less dangerous types of weapons?

ACTIVITY TWO

(This activity can be omitted if time is short.)

Caring for creation

You will need a football or a plastic beach ball and some self-adhesive labels.

Each person in the room has to choose to be either a particular civilization (eg Roman, Greek, American, Arab) or a particular period in history. One person is 'God' and another is 'Today' and a third is 'The next generation'.

Everybody (except 'The next generation' and 'God') needs a label and has to write on the label at least one thing that their civilization contributed to the world.

The person who is 'God' throws the ball to the first of the civilizations and says, 'I am handing you a world, pass it on'. The first person catches the ball and sticks the label on it. Then he or she repeats the sentence 'God' said, throwing the ball to someone else. And so the ball travels around the group until it reaches the person called 'Today'. This person will need a large label as this is the subject we know most about. The rest of the group can call out suggestions for what our present age has contributed to the world, both good and ill. The large label is then stuck on to the ball.

The person who is 'Today' has to decide whether to throw the ball on to 'The next generation' or back to 'God'. Either way, the last person to get the ball reads out all the labels. Use these and the following questions as the basis of a discussion.

God gave humanity a world. What state are we returning it in? What sort of condition will it be in to hand on to the next generation?

Think about it . . .

The weapons we now possess – nuclear, biological and chemical – are aimed at the core of life itself. People have always killed each other in large numbers, but now we can affect unborn generations and the environment on an unprecedented scale. We have technology that can destroy us and our environment; we also have the technology to do tremendous good. For the first time in history we can choose not just what sort of future we have, but whether there will be a future at all. Political and military leaders carry an enormous burden of responsibility as they try to assess what the real threats to their nations are, and how best to counter them.

Note: This section has deliberately emphasized the problems of a technology out of control. Later we shall be looking at the constructive side of defence technology, the resistance of tyranny.

6
LOVE AND PUNISHMENT

6.1 LOVE IS . . .

'Love' is one of those words we all use a lot but seldom stop to think what it means. In our society, 'love' covers everything from heaven to Hollywood. Jesus commanded his followers to 'love' their enemies. What did he mean?

ACTIVITY ONE

'Love is . . .'
Draw a 'Love is' cartoon, representing one aspect of love. Display the cartoons around the room.

Think about it . . .
Even this short activity shows that the word 'love' covers a variety of meanings. The activity below may help to clarify what we mean when we use the word 'love'.

ACTIVITY TWO

Love or love?
Go through the following statements and decide what the word 'love' means in each. Replace the word 'love' in each case with another word or phrase.

1 I love chips.
2 I love swimming.
3 I love . . .; he/she is so sexy.
4 I love my family.
5 I love my country.
6 I love . . . football team.
7 I love my girlfriend/boyfriend.
8 People should love the person they are married to.
9 I fell in love.
10 I stopped loving him/her.
11 They made love.
12 He didn't behave in a loving fashion.

Look at the range of words used to replace love. Are they all related, or are they different?

Think about it . . .
In our society love is often regarded as a feeling and little more. Love comes and goes and is almost regarded as out of our control, like catching measles. Love is given as an excuse for behaviour that we would find difficult to tolerate under other circumstances. For example, unfaithfulness and the breaking of promises are sometimes considered fair means in the cause of love. We have a saying, 'All's fair in love and war'. That is, anything goes. If you're in love or at war there are no rules.

In English, we only have the one word for love, whereas the Bible has many. The Bible's idea of love is very different from that of our society. Paul gave a detailed description of love in 1 Corinthians 13. We need to look at this description of love if we are going to understand what Jesus meant when he said 'Love your enemies'.

CHECK OUT THE BIBLE

Below are some reflections on the different aspects of love spoken in 1 Corinthians 13.

The sections can be used as the basis for a meditation. First, read the whole of 1 Corinthians 13 to the group, then work through the sections, with a number of people taking turns at reading the verses and the comments.

Between sections, and at other natural breaks in the comment, allow times of quiet for personal thought and prayer. For example, after hearing verse 4 read aloud, and the comments on it, one group member may wish to ask God's forgiveness for a particular occasion when they deliberately made someone else look small in order to boost their own image. Another may want to ask God for help in coping with real feelings of jealousy. These prayers would all, of course, be offered silently.

1 Love is what gives life value. (1 Corinthians 13:1-3)

I can say all the right things, know all the right things, even do all the right things – to the extent of sacrificing my own life for a good cause. But if I do it all to get myself a good reputation, rather than out of concern for others, it is worthless.

But for the other side of the coin, read James 2:14-26. The *attitude* of being loving must express itself in *actions* in order to qualify as love. Good intentions and right attitudes aren't enough on their own.

How many wars have been caused by lack of love? Evils have been tolerated and nothing done until the situation has spilled over into violence. There are often fine speeches made, and people 'sympathize' with exploited and underprivileged groups, but how much is actually done?

2 'Love is patient, love is kind.' (v 4)

Both of these words carry very weak images in our society. We tend to think of patience as passively sitting back and waiting. And kindness is seen as a rather pathetic, limp sort of goodness. That is not true of patience and kindness in the Bible. The Bible uses the word patience for living in the Now, not always chafing to be on to the next thing. It is bearing with courage what life brings and not trying to escape every unpleasant happening. Most people spend their lives dodging everything they don't like, trying to avoid or get out of every unpleasant situation. Patience means facing up to those situations – although you want them very much to go away – and learning what you can in them. Patience waits for God's timing, and tries to see what *he* is doing in that situation.

● Read James 5:7-8

The farmer is patient, but he is not idle. While he waits for the rains to come, he knows that it is what he does *now* that counts. If he doesn't plant seed while he waits for the rain, the rain won't do him any good when it does come!

Kindness is not weak; kindness is God's love reaching out practically to people. It is being open to others, letting their sorrows and joys become your own. Kindness is getting involved. Kindness is life with the drawbridge down and your sleeves rolled up. Kindness is risky living.

● Read Luke 10:25-37

What did being kind cost the good Samaritan?

does preventative and healing work, trying to prevent strife and trying to heal the damage caused by it.

3 'Love does not envy, it does not boast, it is not proud.' (v 4)

Love is very secure. Jealousy, conceit and pride are all signs of a shaky ego, an ego that needs boosting by constantly drawing attention to itself. Jealousy means drawing things to yourself because you are afraid of other people's friendships, possessions or successes. You feel threatened by them. Love is secure and free enough to let go of people and possessions and to enjoy other people's success.

Love is not conceited. People who are secure don't need to keep boasting and comparing themselves favourably with others.

Love has no room for selfish pride. Pride cripples love because it makes other people feel stupid and worthless. Pride makes people think only of themselves, and reduces their ability to give to others. Pride also distorts the proud person's view of other people. If someone spends all his or her time thinking how wonderful they are, they can't appreciate others.

Love makes people realistic about themselves, not self-righteous. Love looks at others and recognizes them as people made in the image of God. Where there is evil, love doesn't look on with shock and scorn, but realizes that 'There, but for the grace of God, go I'.

● Read Luke 18:9–14; Matthew 7:1–5
The implicit criticism of the Pharisee's attitude, and the command not to judge, do not imply that people should suspend

Patience is always needed in the political realm. We need to be able to see when it is right to act, and we need to know when things just have to be put up with for a while. Wrongs are seldom righted immediately. Patience is not doing nothing; it is working for right even if the ultimate goals are not within sight.

Probably most people feel that the problems of war and peace are so great that it isn't worth doing anything about them. They have an 'all or nothing' mentality. But patience is about getting on with what you can do now, not forever wishing you were in some different situation. Patience is hard work that springs out of a positive attitude of mind. Each of us has been given life and time as gifts; patience says, 'Use *today* to the full to work for tomorrow's peace. Don't always be wishing that tomorrow was already here.'

Kindness describes love in action. It

▶▶

all their critical faculties. Rather, they mean that people have to be very self-aware when exercising judgment, for all judgments speak both to the person being judged and to the one doing the judging.

Nations can be proud and conceited. National pride has often been used for the wrong ends, to fuel hatred in war. Nations, like individuals, need to be proud of the right things – such as love and justice – rather than propping up their national egos with violence.

4 'Love is not rude, it is not self-seeking, it is not easily angered.' (v 5)

Our society is a self-seeking one; people are constantly told to assert their rights. Soap operas are full of people who seek revenge because they feel they don't have what is theirs by rights. Ours is an assertive society, but for the Christian, rights are only asserted in order to serve the truth, to serve justice and to serve others.

Rudeness and irritability equally stem from selfishness. People become irritable and rude when they feel cheated out of something they thought was theirs, whether that is money, time, or a relationship. If self is at the centre it is constantly frustrated and irritable.

● Read John 13:12–17
Jesus came to serve others, so that he could show them how much God cares for them. He didn't come insisting on his own rights. Genuine love puts God at the centre, and not self. And that is a major revolution.

How often do nations stand on their rights (the right to a certain standard of living, for example, or to particular resources) at the expense of others? Politics can become a power struggle between the rights of different groups. 'Rights' need to be carefully assessed in the light of love and justice. Whose rights should be taken notice of? Whose should be given up for the sake of others?

Nations are as self-assertive as individuals; it would be a brave nation that looked to the needs of others as well as to its own. This may sound very idealistic, but a major study was published in 1980 on the discrepancy in living standards between the wealthy northern hemisphere and the poorer south. The report, called *North-South: A Programme for Survival* and known as the Brandt Report, concluded that a fairer policy towards the south would be good for everyone, economically and politically. Fairer trading policies with poorer countries might be the place where love, justice and politics can join hands. Love is not always bad politics.

5 'Love keeps no record of wrongs. Love does not delight in evil but rejoices with the truth.' (vs 5–6)

Love doesn't keep a record of wrongs; it doesn't insist on keeping scores or putting the record straight. Love lets the past die and doesn't allow itself to become bitter.

Love hates evil and does not try to pretend that corrupt people are really good. Rather, it tries to stop such people from doing evil. Love hates the sin but loves the sinner; it can get tough as only real love can. Tough love will not allow the sinner to carry on in sin. If we really care, we will not allow a person to be trapped in evil. Take the example of a child with a bad temper who keeps on hitting out. Is it kind to let him remain like that? He will remain trapped inside aggression which will have disastrous ▶▶

▶▶

social consequences for him in the future. He will have few friends and his uncontrolled temper will damage his enjoyment of life. A loving parent will seek to channel and control that temper.

● Read Proverbs 3:12

It is not easy, and some would say it is not valid, to move from the force used to control a child to the force used in war. The principle may stand, however, that sometimes love has to get tough. This principle does not, of course, open the door to the use of unlimited force – either to control a child, or in war.

How many wars have been not only started but prolonged because nations have long memories? The vicious circle of revenge is difficult to break. Listen to the news for half an hour and see how many cases of violence are the result of deep-seated bitterness caused by past wrongs. Love lets the past go and forgives in spite of it.

6 'Love always protects, always trusts, always hopes, always perseveres.' (v 7)

Love protects those who cannot protect themselves. It bears the other person's burden.

Love is a bit careless, and is secure enough not to mind occasionally being taken for a ride. It isn't thick or stupid because it lets this happen, but love stops people becoming cynical and despairing. Love is not hard.

Love carries on hoping when all looks hopeless because a Christian's hope for the future is placed in God, and he doesn't let you down, break promises or disappoint.

● Read Matthew 10:16

Sheep are vulnerable and easily hurt. Most people, when they get hurt, withdraw or harden up. Neither of these are options for the Christian. What do you think 'be as shrewd as snakes and as innocent as doves' means in relation to 1 Corinthians 13:7?

Christians are called to be wise, but not hard; to use their common sense, but to remain open and vulnerable. If people ever get to the point where they cannot be hurt, something has gone wrong. It leads to cynicism and a feeling of helplessness. Love does not give up, and cynicism and hardness are not options open to the Christian. Jesus sent his followers out warning them that they would be like 'sheep among wolves'; but he didn't advise them to become like thick-skinned rhinoceroses in self-defence!

7 'Love never fails.' (v 8)

Love outlasts everything because it is the nature of God himself. There is nothing weak about love; love is tough on evil and gets involved. It gets hurt and then goes back and tries again. Love doesn't stop just because it isn't getting results; it does what is right even if it doesn't change the world.

● Read 1 John 4:7–8

'God is love' means that we can say what love is by describing God's character. Christians must look carefully at how they love; and must use God, not their own society, as a model for what love is.

In most areas of life, people do, of course, try to see what the results of their action will be. But as we have already noted, in the area of war and peace most people do nothing because they feel their actions won't make the slightest bit of difference to the total situation. You may *not* change the world, but there are certain things that are right and loving to do ▶▶

regardless of their national or global results. Love is persistent in the face of apparently no positive results because it is not working on the basis of results alone. Like the boy with the five loaves and two fish, sometimes Christians have to give what little they have and leave the rest to God. People spend so much time on things that don't last, things that will die with them. Love lasts; time and energy put into love is never wasted.

● Read Matthew 25:37–40 for the value God places on practical love.

● Read 1 Corinthians 3:10–14
Think of the sort of things you spend your time on. Are they the sort of things that will last?

Think about it . . .

'Love' in the Bible is not sentimental. When Jesus called his disciples to love their enemies he was talking about something very different from nice feelings. Love is hard work. Luther, the great sixteenth-century Reformer, called war 'the strange work of love', the moment when love has to get tough with injustice. Christians agree that love does not exclude getting tough but they begin to disagree with each other about whether taking life is sometimes a necessary part of getting tough. You will have to decide for yourself whether love can ever mean that a Christian has to take life in defence of right and to stop evil. It is not necessarily outside the boundaries of love to do so. When Christians who are not pacifists fight alongside their neighbours against an evil government or regime, they do not believe they step outside the commandment of love; rather they believe they are acting out of love both for the victim and also for the aggressor.

6.2 GETTING WHAT YOU DESERVE

When making decisions about war and pacifism, the fact has to be faced that the human race is not perfect. Christians believe there is a bias towards wrong in humanity which they label sin. This is a fact which has to be faced. It is not popular in our society to talk about sin but one glance at the news ought to be enough to convince people that humanity is flawed. Facing up to the existence of sin doesn't turn Christians into hard and cynical pessimists, rather it keeps them realistic about what can be achieved. It is because people are flawed that nations find it difficult to trust each other. It is sin that makes it necessary to have adequate means of verifying treaties, in order to make sure that neither side 'cheats'. The basic cause of all our planet's problems was known centuries ago – see Jeremiah 17:9.

There is evil within the human heart but there is good there as well. This world was created by a good God and still bears his trade mark.

Any decision about war must take full account of human sinfulness. There will be no heaven on earth, no Utopia. Sin and evil are a fact of life this side of heaven and must figure in decision-making. This fact of life affects everything we do, as the following activity shows.

ACTIVITY ONE

Whizz . . . bang!
Think through the normal activities of the day, the things you do and the people you meet. Now imagine that the human race has suddenly become perfect. How would your day be different?

Think about it . . .
Pacifists are often accused of not taking sin seriously enough. That is not always true: some pacifists take sin very seriously indeed. Many pacifists recognize that appalling evil would descend on a nation that renounced the use of force against an invading army. But they measure this against the equally appalling loss of life caused by war. Those who take a different view and allow the use of 'lethal force' feel that, if necessary, sin must be kept in check by the legitimate use of force. They believe that sin, by its very nature, will not check itself, but will just get worse if allowed to. Churchill summed up this view when he said that men's hearts must be ruled by fear until they are ruled by love.

CHECK OUT THE BIBLE

● Read Romans 6:23

Our society has a mixed view of judgment and punishment. On the one hand, people are very keen to see long prison sentences imposed on violent criminals, and many seem in favour of bringing back the death penalty. But often, these same people can't imagine that *God* would ever think of judging or punishing evil. But the Bible clearly portrays God as a judge, and shows that sin does bring punishment.

● Read Isaiah 3:13–15

Judgment and punishment are closely tied to justice. If justice is to be done to the poor and the oppressed that means making judgments on oppressors.

Evil is not tolerated in the Bible, neither is it ignored. But it is not only amongst Christians and religious people that a sense of right and wrong is found.

People have a basic sense of morality. Most people think it is wrong to murder. Most people do not want the guilty to go free, or the innocent to suffer. The Bible assumes a basic sense of right and wrong among mankind (see Romans 2:14–15).

Even in war people are held morally responsible for their behaviour. After the Second World War certain Nazis were tried as war criminals; common humanity made the judgment that even the extremities of war did not excuse the atrocities that had been committed. The Nuremberg trials were a passing of judgment; there was something abhorrent about allowing such people to go through life thinking – however sincerely – that they were right. Judgment and punishment make sense of life. They show that what people do, matters. They give meaning to actions.

ACTIVITY TWO

Punishment and authority

Write the following on pieces of paper:

1 Smack a child
2 Declare war
3 End the world
4 Give a detention
5 Sack workers
6 Drop a bomb
7 Stop pocket money
8 Put people in prison
9 Ban a protest
10 Fine someone

Place the pieces of paper face down on the floor. Copy the following on pieces of paper, a different colour from the previous list:

1 Parent
2 Prime Minister
3 President
4 Magistrate
5 Teacher
6 Employer
7 God
8 Judge
9 Police officer
10 Grandparent

Place these face down on the floor.

People should pick two pieces of paper at random, one of each colour. The pair should be read out and the group should decide whether that 'punishment' is appropriate to that person's authority. For example:

Authority: Teacher
Punishment: Declare war

Think about it . . .

This activity illustrates that certain types of judgment are appropriate to certain people. This is not a double standard but arises from the belief that God has given different groups the authority to use differing degrees of force.

WAR AS PUNISHMENT

Judgment and punishment are important concepts but judgment is a prerogative of God which he sometimes delegates to certain human beings. In Romans 13:1–7 the state is given the power to punish the wrongdoer. In the Old Testament, God uses nations to punish others through war.

The question that is relevant here is, should war still be used today as a means of judging evil nations? If God in the New Testament gave the state the power to judge wrongdoers, does that right stop at the national boundary? Is God inhibited by geography?

In the second activity we examined the problem of who has the power to execute different judgments. In the Old Testament the emphasis is fairly strongly on God judging the nations through Israel or another nation. In the New Testament the emphasis is even more strongly on God being the judge. There are very strong warnings on people judging individually; (see, for example, Matthew 7:1–5). Making judgments and meting out punishment is, however, part of the duty

of the state. What is questionable is the use of war by any single nation today *as an instrument of judgment* on another.

WAR AS A PREVENTATIVE MEASURE

Generally today, war is used as a preventative measure rather than as a means of judging a nation.

There are several reasons for this:

1 No nation today is the equivalent of Old Testament Israel. In the New Testament the church takes its place, and the church is world-wide.
2 It is difficult for nations to act without a strong bias in favour of their own culture. People tend to gloss over the evils at home and magnify those abroad. The West might abhor communism and think it worth going to war over; other nations might think our affluence and lack of morality obscene and come to a similar conclusion.
3 The weapons nations now possess often make it inappropriate to go to war because we could be making a far bigger judgment than the situation warrants; wars can easily escalate. The punishments inflicted are often inappropriate to the office held or the original offence.

Having made these provisos, there are extreme cases where countries have been invaded on humanitarian grounds in order to end an oppressive, tyrannical regime. But this is not so much with the aim of punishing the oppressor, as relieving the real and desperate need of the oppressed. Such interventions are not self-righteous but the moral response of fellow human beings. Force is the last resort, not the first option. There is a strong call for justice in the Bible but justice, like charity, begins at home. In certain desperate situations, need it stop there?

Think about it . . .

The decision you have to make is whether under any circumstances war can ever be used as an instrument of judgment by a nation or whether that has to be left to God. Some Christians would use force when intervention on humanitarian grounds is called for and, secondarily, to punish an evil regime. Other Christians will use all other means short of war.

All Christians agree that any form of judgment must start with themselves and work outwards. An unloving church cannot make judgments on an unloving society, and one unloving society cannot judge another.

7
BIG BROTHER

In Romans 13:1–7 and in the Old Testament the state is given the power to take life. The questions arise for the Christian:

1 Does this include war?
2 Should the Christian help the state in this task?
3 Has a Christian the right to withhold help and co-operation from the state?
4 Can the state authorize an individual to take life, when it would be wrong for that individual to do so on his own authority?
5 Pacifists take the example of Jesus and apply it to the behaviour of all Christians and the state. So, similarly, can't the command to the state to use the sword to punish evil within its boundaries also be widened to apply to war outside its boundaries?

HOW FAR CAN THE STATE GO?

The Bible sees the state as having certain powers, but they are restricted.

The state is not above the law, rather it is judged by God's law. If the state steps outside its God-given role and tries to claim for itself power that belongs to God alone, it may be disobeyed. Too often the statements about the authority of the state in Romans and 1 Peter have led Christians to accept injustice and tyranny, as the article in the appendix illustrates. The state's authority is derived from God, and obedience to it must be balanced by a Christian critique of the state's behaviour and, if necessary, protest and rejection of the state's claims.

Think of some situations where it would be right to disobey the state. (The passages below may help.)

CHECK OUT THE BIBLE

● Read Daniel 3:1–6, 13–18 and Acts 4:16–20.
How had the state stepped outside its authority in both these cases?

The state's function is to keep law and order and provide a framework within which love and justice can operate. The state, or government, exists to serve the people in its care, not for its own sake. The state also serves to keep evil in check; if ever the state aligns itself with evil then it must be challenged.

All human authority ultimately comes from God, it is a derived authority, not an absolute one. For the Christian there can be no blind obedience to human authority.

● Read Daniel 5:1–6, 22–28; and John 19:11.
Both Pilate and Belshazzar failed to realize that their authority came from God – with his instructions for how to use it.

● Read Romans 13:1–7; and 1 Peter 2:13–17.
These verses outline the limits of the state's authority. It is there to protect its citizens and to enable them to live in peace together. It is to act as 'God's servant', rewarding those citizens who do good and punishing those who do wrong. The implication of this is that when a state ceases to do these things it will be using the power God has given it for wrong purposes.

▶▶

▶▶

In both of these passages the state referred to was Rome, a state that became very hostile to Christianity. Christians were told to submit to the state but we know from history that they disobeyed it when it tried to force them to do wrong.

Christians refused to sacrifice to the emperor and they generally did not join the army, though it is not clear whether this was solely on pacifist grounds or because of the idolatry involved in serving in the army.

Think about it . . .

For Christians there is only one absolute allegiance, that is their loyalty to God. They are loyal to the state in so far as the state administrates God's justice, love and orderliness, and does not ask its citizens to put aside that greater loyalty. It is hardly surprising that Christians in the past have been seen as subversive! The Christian has to maintain a delicate balance between obedience to the authorities, so far as is possible, and resistance if the state steps outside of its God-given role.

TWO CHRISTIAN VIEWS OF THE STATE

We have looked briefly at the power of the state, but we can see that Christians have, since the very beginning of the church, taken up two main positions, one positive and one negative. These two positions are the two ends of the spectrum, there are of course a variety of positions that lie in the middle.

Think about the following two views of the function of the state. For each, discuss how the daily life of a person holding that view would be affected by it.

View 1

1 The state has a God-given role to protect its citizens, to reward good and punish evil.
2 Force is legitimately exercised by the state for this purpose.

3 Romans 13:1–7 and 1 Peter 2:13–17 refer to policing activities by the state. It may be applied to the state's role in the international scene, as well as within its own territory.
4 Power is a tool that can be used for good or ill. Christians should be actively involved in the state's use of power, to ensure that it is used for good.
5 God uses the state as an instrument of justice. The state may actively co-operate with God in bringing about justice in the world.
6 This is a basically optimistic view of the state.

View 2

1 The state has a God-given role to protect its citizens, to reward good and punish evil.
2 It is not legitimate for a Christian to co-operate with the state's use of force, even when for this purpose. God has given that task to the state, not to the church. Christians are called to live differently as the church, as a witness to the state.
3 Romans 13 and 1 Peter 2:13–17 refer only to policing activities within the state. They cannot be extended to apply to war.
4 Power is not a neutral tool that can be wielded either for good or ill by the state. It is something easily perverted to evil ends. Too often the state actually perpetrates evil instead of restraining it.
5 God may use the state as an

instrument of judgment, but that does not mean God approves of all that the state does. The state is not always consciously co-operating with God's purposes.

6 This is a basically pessimistic view of the state.

Each view has practical consequences for the person who holds it .

The Christian who holds view 1:
● will aid the state in its God-given task of upholding justice within the state. He or she could be a policeman/woman, for instance.
● will be prepared to obey the state's command to prepare for war (if he considers the cause just) – making weapons, for example – or to actually fight in a war. The Christian could be a soldier.

Christians who hold view 1 often attempt to 'Christianize' the state; that is, they work for the development of Christian values and principles within the state.

The Christian who holds view 2:
● recognizes that the state is entitled to defend itself and lets it get on with its task, but does not help it. Certain pacifists believe that God often uses individuals or states to carry out his purposes, although he may not approve of their actions. For example, God used Babylon to punish Israel, but that does not mean he approved of all that Babylon did.
● may believe that people should not try to Christianize the state from within; that is, they should not try to make a largely non-Christian state behave according to Christian morality. Rather, Christians should set up a radical alternative, a peaceful way of living that will witness to the state. Many pacifists will act in 'non-combatant' roles, serving as ambulance personnel or in the medical services, but will not serve directly in the armed forces.

The state's job is not easy; ordered government is something to be grateful for and to pray for (1 Timothy 2:1–4). In order to see a little of some of the hard decisions that have to be made, try the following activity if there is time.

ACTIVITY ONE

Declaring independence
Your group has just declared independence. If you like, issue passports to the members. As a newly independent state there are several things to be decided.

1 How are you going to come to decisions?
2 Do you need a leader? If so, decide how the leader is going to be chosen and appoint one by using the method you decide.
3 How are you going to make laws?
4 Decide on ten basic laws for your country.
5 What are you going to do when someone breaks the law?
6 Are people who disagree with the leader or the government going to be able to voice their objections? If so, what are they allowed to do?
7 What will your country do in the following situations:
● You are the victims of an unprovoked

attack from another country.
- There is a massacre going on in a neighbouring country.
- A group of people within your own country is suffering persecution at the hands of others.

Think about it . . .

It is easy to decide right and wrong in the abstract. It is much harder when you find yourself in the real situation. All the situations described in the last activity have happened within recent history.

Belgium and Holland had not provoked Hitler. India went to the aid of Eastern Pakistan when there were terrible massacres in that country. German Jews and communists were put in concentration camps long before Hitler turned his attention to the outside world.

ACTIVITY TWO

Law and the Christian

Look at the basic laws you made for your country. Would Christians be happy obeying them? Would some Christians feel they would have to disobey?

Below are a few laws. Decide as a group whether you could or couldn't obey them as Christians.

1 Everybody should spend three years in the army.
2 There should be corporal punishment (flogging) for certain offences.
3 Everybody should have the freedom to worship, whatever religion they belong to; but no one should have the right to evangelize (spread their faith).
4 People who disagree with the state should be put in camps and 're-educated'.
5 All sermons should be checked by the government.

6 There should be no form of state welfare for the poor; this should be provided on a voluntary basis by the churches.
7 The police should all be armed.
8 People of a different colour from the majority should live in restricted areas.
9 Disabled people and the elderly should be killed in a humane fashion when they are no longer useful to the state.
10 People of different religion from the majority should have restricted rights.

Think about it . . .

Some of the above laws are in force in different countries today, but Christians do not all start violent revolutions because of them. Those of us who live in democracies and have the channels for peaceful change have a duty to use them. They are rights our ancestors never had and which we may lose one day if we do not exercise them. Many of the revolutions of the past have been caused because there were no avenues for peaceful change. Christians certainly have a duty to keep such avenues for change open.

Revolution against the state is an even more difficult issue for the Christian than taking part in a properly declared war. Most Christians feel very uneasy about violent revolution but some feel that they are left with no alternative.

It is easy to condemn revolution but history often shows that the freedoms that are enjoyed now are a result of it. Some Christians believe that in extreme circumstances the government has to be resisted by force; others will use only peaceful means.

History carries warnings about violent revolution; sometimes violence breeds violence. And how often has the liberating revolution itself become oppressive?

8
MIGHT AND RIGHT

8.1 THE RULES OF THE GAME

Many Christians believe, often with great reluctance, that right sometimes needs defending by force of arms. This has been an accepted Christian position since the fourth century although Christians have never felt happy about using force. Even during the Middle Ages there was the feeling that war was deeply at variance with the gospel. Priests did not fight and there was penance and confession for those who did.

'ALL'S FAIR IN LOVE AND WAR'

It has long been recognized that 'War is hell'. We mentioned earlier the saying, 'All's fair in love and war'. We have the idea that in extreme circumstances the normal laws of morality do not bind us. Christians who support the defence of right by use of arms reject this idea and, since the fourth century, have tried to insist on certain 'rules of war'.

ACTIVITY ONE

Handicap
Two people sit on the floor, back to back with their legs together flat on the floor in front of them, and their hands on their knees. On the signal to start, both people turn around and try to pin the shoulders of their opponent to the floor for three seconds. They may use their hands. Neither participant is allowed to rise from their knees, and the contest lasts for one minute.

Try this again with another pair of opponents. This time one person has one hand tied behind his back. What happens?

ALTERNATIVE ACTIVITY

Play the game
Bring in some board games to play. Spend a few minutes playing these games with friends then ask one person to abandon the rules. What happens to the game?

Think about it . . .
Rules enable us to predict the opponent's moves. They give both players a framework to play within as long as both players stick to the rules, as the activity above shows. War is often depicted as a game without rules but Christians (and many others) insist that even in the most extreme situation of war we are still to obey certain laws. War does not excuse any sort of behaviour. The 'rules of war' are sometimes described as 'fighting with your hands tied'. Rules are fine as long as both parties stick to them, but if one party doesn't, the other one is at a tremendous disadvantage.

For example, there are advantages in using torture; you gain information which may enable you to win. Winning is important, particularly against an evil tyrant, but a prisoner of war is also one of God's people and must be treated as such. The ends do not justify the use of *any* means; it is important to fight 'well' if we have to fight at all. This is not only true from the point of view of Christian morality; a nation also needs to think of the long-term future – how it will come to terms with the war afterwards and what will be the effect on the population of the methods used.

This all sounds fine, but it is written in a time of peace and we all know that in the extremity of war decisions about such things are hard to make. The situation is far more complex and difficult than I have indicated, but the principle holds: it is important to win, but it is also important *how* you win. Most of us will not have to make such decisions and it must be borne in mind that if a war was important enough to enter into in the first place, winning must be very important indeed.

For example, at the end of World War Two the allies tried certain Nazi 'war criminals' for their crimes against humanity. Even in the event of a world war we held people responsible. Ordinary people (not just Christians) felt that there were certain things that soldiers should not do, even in war. Attacks on non-combatants, torture and massacre were not excusable.

This happened again in Vietnam. After the My Lai massacre there was a trial: it was not enough for the soldiers to say they were following orders; they were deemed responsible for their actions and treated accordingly.

THE JUST WAR THEORY

For many years Christians have used what is called 'The Just War Theory'. This is not an exclusively Christian set of rules but many of the ideas are based on biblical principles. Below are some of the terms by which a war is considered 'just'.

(Either write out all these points on an OHP slide, so that all the group can see them; or give each group member a photocopy of the list as presented here.)

1 War can only be declared if there is a just cause. War is not an instrument of policy or retaliation; it is not a means of spreading religious or political ideology.

The Bible puts a strong emphasis on justice, see Amos 5:24.

2 The intention must be just: it must be to restore a just peace.

The desire for, and promise of, world-wide peace is a strong element in the Bible, in both the Old Testament and the New. See, for instance, Isaiah 9:5–7.

3 It must be as a last resort, when everything else has failed. The taking of life was never a casual affair in the Bible – see Deuteronomy 20:10.

4 There must be an official declaration of war by a legitimate power.

5 Limited objectives must be set. There must not be a refusal to settle for anything less than unconditional surrender. The economy of the enemy must not be destroyed.

Total destruction either of the economy or a people was not allowed in the Bible. The next generation was preserved and the economy protected. See, for instance, Amos 1:13; Deuteronomy 20:19–20.

6 The immunity of non-combatants

must be respected. Innocent life is protected in the Bible: see Genesis 18:23–33.

7 Limited means must be used in proportion to the objectives you want to achieve; in other words, you don't take a hammer to crack an egg!

8 There must be a reasonable hope of success when you start; don't start a war you can't win.

9 The benefit from the war must outweigh the evil of going to war. You don't go to war over trivial matters.

10 There must be scope for conscientious objectors to opt out of the war.

In one particular instance in the Bible, even those who were only 'faint-hearted' could leave the army: Judges 7:3 (see also Deuteronomy 20:8).

Think about it . . .

Some of the just war theory is specifically Christian, other parts of it are less so.

For example, sometimes Christians would want to oppose wrong even if they saw little hope of success. Sometimes Christians would want to defend right even if a large number of people were not involved.

Question

Can the just war theory work in a nuclear age? In answering this consider some of the points listed below.

PROBLEMS WITH THE JUST WAR THEORY

1 Nuclear, biological and chemical weapons are indiscriminate *by design*. That means they deliberately kill the innocent.

2 It is very difficult in modern warfare to decide who is non-combatant. Factory workers supply the army with clothes and other equipment; our taxes provide the money for weapons.

3 The destructive effect of nuclear weapons is so great that it would be out of proportion to any good the winning side might achieve. There are smaller nuclear weapons that can be aimed more precisely, but what would stop their use escalating?

4 The problems a country would have after a nuclear hit are so vast that the concept of 'winning' a war becomes absurd.

5 The state that holds fast to the just war theory tends to be fighting with its hands behind its back.

Think about it . . .

The record of the just war theory has not been good, even in conventional warfare, but it is an honest attempt to curb the brutality of war. This theory needs rewriting for the nuclear age. We can't just take the theories of the past and apply them as they stand to modern warfare. When nuclear weapons were first invented Albert Einstein made the comment that everything had changed – except our thinking. It is time now for our thinking to change too. The just war theory is no cop-out for Christians – it is a serious attempt to bring every area of life under moral judgment – but it has to be recognized that we live in a new age for which we need new rules.

8.2 YOU HIT ME AND I'LL HIT YOU BACK!

THE MORALITY OF NUCLEAR DETERRENCE

For nearly forty years the West has known 'peace'. This has been put down to the deterrent effect of nuclear weapons. Nuclear weapons have held a kind of 'balance of terror'. For the first time in history war has become unthinkable. Our policies and our weapons are now largely designed to avoid war. The deterrent effect of weapons is nothing new; it was said by Vegetius in the fourth century, 'Let him who desires peace, prepare for war'. Many people maintain that nuclear weapons have held the peace, and that a type of stability has been reached which relies on terror and psychological stalemate. The very weapons that threaten life itself, preserve life. So out of this terrible evil some good has come; nuclear weapons are so terrible that we dare not use them! Indeed, even conventional weapons are used cautiously in case the fighting escalates.

Nuclear weapons have stripped war of all its false glory. War is now seen to be the bloody cruelty it has always been to its victims. It has taken weapons as terrible as those we now possess to bring humanity to its senses. Those in possession of nuclear weapons cannot lightly go to war.

There is however another view. The possession of an increasing number of nuclear weapons for deterrence is seen by some as 'nuclear madness'. Such a policy may have been plausible with other types of weapons but with such potentially destructive weapons it is unthinkable. As Arthur Koestler has said, 'Hitherto man has had to live with the idea of death as an individual; from now onward, mankind will have to live with the idea of death as a species' (quoted in *The Pilgrim's Guide to the New Age* by A and S Lawhead, Lion, 1986).

The *Pax Atomica* is a very fragile peace. It may be all the peace that our world can know. Are there any alternatives? If not, is there any way that a Christian can subscribe to the policy of deterrence with a clean conscience?

Think about it . . .

Before you can answer any of these questions some groundwork needs to be done, and some other questions need to be answered. Use these as a basis for discussion.

1 Are nuclear weapons wrong in themselves or are they wrong because of their consequences? The answer to this is important because, if these weapons are wrong in themselves, then Christians should have nothing to do with them; even possessing them would be wrong.

2 What are people actually intending when they have nuclear weapons? Are they intending to kill millions of people by threatening another nation? Or is the prime intention to keep the peace? Or is there a double intention? If the prime intention *is* to kill by the million then Christians must say that is wrong.

3 If the prime intention is to deter aggression are nuclear weapons necessarily wrong?

ACTIVITY ONE

To destroy, or to deter?

Draw two large circles on a sheet of paper. In one write 'destructive weapon', in the other write 'deterrent'. Write 'nuclear weapons' in both.

What other things would you class with nuclear weapons in each set? Locks and bolts deter the burglar; would they go in the set marked 'deter'? The policeman's gun is a weapon; would that go in the set marked 'destructive weapon'?

Think about it . . .

This is a very difficult area. You probably discovered during the activity that it is very difficult to separate an action from its consequences. People don't agree over whether nuclear weapons are inherently evil; there are a variety of positions that people take (a secret ballot can be taken to see how many of the group agree with each of these views):

1 Nuclear weapons are inherently evil and Christians should have nothing to do with them, regardless of the consequences.

2 Nuclear weapons are evil but Christians cannot disregard the consequences of abandoning them. Christians may have to abandon their innocence and use one evil to stop another.

3 Nuclear weapons are no more evil than any other weapon of war. People have killed each other by the million before, even with swords. Nuclear weapons are part of the development of weaponry, not necessarily a different class of weapon.

4 Nuclear weapons are all right as long as we never intend to use them. They are neutral, neither good nor bad; their moral standing – like a stick – can only be determined by the use to which they are put. Sticks can be used to build a fire or to hit someone; it is the intention of the user that counts.

You will have to decide for yourself whether nuclear weapons are wrong in themselves, or whether it is the use they are put to that counts. This brings us to the point of discussing the morality of intention. Is deterrence one big bluff or would we really use these weapons if the occasion arose? Are nuclear weapons an effective deterrent unless other countries think they really will be used?

ACTIVITY TWO

Call my bluff

(Select three people for the 'call my bluff' team, one week in advance. Let them have the instructions, and give them the week to prepare their cases).

Three people need a shoe box each and they should write on the outside the name of a type of weapon. Two of the weapons can be entirely fictitious, but they must sound plausible. The third must be a real weapon. Each person should be able to speak about their weapon for thirty seconds.

Each person has inside the shoe box a piece of paper saying either 'true' or 'false'. Only one person can have a piece of paper saying 'true'; the others must be 'false'.

Each person must talk for thirty seconds as convincingly as they can about their weapon, stressing how deadly it is. The panel of three can be questioned by the rest of the group, then the group has to come to a decision about who has the real weapon. That person then shows the group his card, revealing whether they made the right decision.

The above is a well-known game that people have played for years, and this is how some people think about deterrence. Deterrence is viewed as a sophisticated game of 'call my bluff' played with deadly weapons, but in this case it is the panel which does the guessing. They are not trying to decide which of the others has them but who is likely to use them.

THE MORALITY OF BLUFF

Bluff, if it is true bluff, means that people really never intend to use these weapons. If that is true, it means that whole populations, armies and scientists are all fooled, for bluff only works if you are thoroughly convincing; the enemy must believe you. Only a few at the very top would be in on the secret that these weapons were never to be used.

Jesus had something to say about truth. Engaging in such a bluff would certainly be morally difficult for a Christian.

● Read Matthew 5:33–37
Would Jesus' words on truthfulness apply to bluff, or does this have to be weighed against the greater evil of war?

THE POWER OF LIFE AND DEATH

There is another problem for the Christian. With the invention of atomic weapons and the harnessing of nuclear power, mankind can threaten the very sources of life itself: we can now destroy everything on this planet that allows life to continue. The arguments that now have to come into play are not those for or against war, but those used to decide about suicide, abortion and euthanasia. Are we usurping God's role by taking for ourselves the power to destroy this world? We like to think of ourselves as rational, grown-up and responsible, but is any human being 'grown-up' enough to be in charge of such powers? Human beings with such powers may be more like kids playing catch with a grenade with the pin out.

ACTIVITY THREE

The red button

Put a circle of red paper in the middle of the floor, and stand one person on it. The rest of the group should write on pieces of paper the qualities they would like to see in the person in charge of the nuclear button. They should pin these qualities to the person standing on the paper.

Read out all the qualities the group suggests. Can you think of any world figure who has all of those qualities? Can you think of world figures you would not want in charge of the button? It is because the power wielded by a nuclear state is so deadly that there are many checks and balances on the power of the rulers, particularly within democracies.

Think about it . . .

This whole section is full of difficult questions on which you will have to make up your own mind. Here are the main ones:

1 Are nuclear weapons wrong in themselves?
2 Is the very threat of their use wrong, even if it is a bluff?
3 Do nuclear weapons increase stability or decrease it?

The most vital question is **1**. Your answer to this will affect your answers to the others. If you believe that nuclear weapons are not wrong in themselves, you have less difficulty in keeping them. If you believe that they *are* wrong, then there are two courses open to you:

a. Get rid of them straight away.
b. Go for a reduction in weapons and a limited deterrence, recognizing that you will be involved in something you don't believe is right, but believing you have little alternative in the face of the reality of evil.

If you believe that having nuclear weapons creates stability then it would make sense to go for 'maximum deterrence', accumulating more weapons in order to balance the enemy's weapons. If you believe that nuclear weapons create instability, then a weapons reduction and slow phasing out or unilateral disarmament would follow.

There are no easy answers to this problem, and there are no answers that leave a Christian with clean hands and a pure conscience. We have invented nuclear weapons and cannot wipe out that knowledge. The responsibility for what we do with them now, and for how we use that knowledge further, lies firmly with us.

9
OPTIONS

9.1 COUNTING THE COST

Whatever position you take over the issues we have looked at so far, there are prices to be paid. This section will be looking at some of the costs involved in the main options.

(The three options could be prepared in advance by three individuals or small groups, and then presented by them to the rest of the group.)

1 PACIFISM

Pacifism is a blanket word for there are many different types of pacifists. Some people are total pacifists and don't believe in any use of force or coercion. Others believe in the minimal use of force within the state by the police force, but believe an unacceptable moral boundary has been crossed once a state goes to war.

Fighting without weapons

Pacifism is not a soft option, for pacifists are not passive. Many pacifists believe in the use of civil disobedience on a national scale to defeat an invader. This sort of fighting starts after the enemy has invaded and the general population – not just the defending army – has become involved in contact with the enemy.

Invading armies rely on communications, the administration and economy of the country they have invaded. It is impossible to run a country when the communications are constantly cut, the railways aren't running and vital pieces of equipment go missing. If the workforce refuses to work, the factories won't run and foreign workers or soldiers have to be imported to do the necessary work. This ties up large sections of the invading army, either working in factories or guarding workers.

You can't arrest a whole nation. The invading army will probably retaliate with mass arrests, torture and killing, but it is difficult to fire on people who never fight back. This sort of defence aims to break the morale of the invading soldiers. It is recognized that there will be massacres, torture and imprisonment. The army would probably try to starve the population into submission.

As well as actively not co-operating, Christian pacifists would meet the enemy with love and forgiveness.

This type of radical love shook the Roman world when it was confronted by Christians who testified to the power of love in action. But it must never be forgotten that the price that the early Christians paid was that of many deaths in the arena, many sent to the salt mines, and constant persecution. There is also the problem that Christian pacifists are a minority in most countries. Can they expect others, who do not necessarily share their convictions, to face national martyrdom? There is nothing glamorous about defence without arms. It is no less bloody than many wars, but all the blood spilt is on one side. The blood spilt is, of course, that of the general population; the ideal advocated by those who believe in 'just' war is the restriction of fighting to the armies alone. There is no certainty of victory, but there is no guarantee of victory in war either.

The cost

1 This means of defence starts after an invasion. However, the possession of weapons may have stopped the invasion occurring in the first place.

2 It is costly in terms of human life, but so is war.

3 It does leave the Christian's conscience free of the guilt of taking life. It doesn't leave the Christian's conscience free of allowing life to be taken.

4 It does not leave a nation in a position to defend others. How does one nation come to the aid of another non-violently?

ACTIVITY ONE

Non-violent resistance

You could probably imagine the use of this type of defence within the school or work situation.

Divide into two groups, either management/workers or pupils/teachers. The management/teachers have to think up some new rules for their workforce/pupils; these can be as strict or hard as they want. The new terms are read out to the workforce/pupils and they then have to try to get the management/teachers to change their minds. Each group should think carefully about the tactics it employs as they do have consequences: the management/teachers have sanctions which they can use against their workers/pupils.

Spend five to ten minutes trying to get each other to back down. At the end, add up the cost to both parties.

Example

New rule: There shall be silence during lunch time.

Response: The pupils held a talk-in in the dining room.

Response: The head refused to have lunch served.

Response: The pupils left the premises in protest.

Response: The head suspended them for the rest of the week.

Response: The pupils wrote to the local paper to bring public pressure to bear on the head and mobilized parents to protest to the Local Education Authority.

Response: Head still refused to back down; would not have the pupils back until they agreed to the new rules.

Response: Pupils took their case to the Minister of Education who was loath to interfere.

Response: The Head was worried about the adverse publicity, and so agreed to have the pupils back if they agreed to abide by the new rule as an interim measure, while new school rules were worked out in conjunction with pupils.

Response: The pupils agreed.

The cost

The cost in this case was high. The cost to the head, in terms of the school's reputation, is incalculable; the cost to the pupils was also high as it was close to their exams and they lost a lot of valuable time. The damage to staff/pupil relations will take years to repair. Was it worth it?

Think about it . . .

Before deciding on any action, people need to count the cost. They need to be realistic about the consequences of their actions. Martin Luther King did not call the black community to civil disobedience over a minor issue; the results of that disobedience were bloody and, for the King family, fatal. The cost of fighting without arms will be counted in the dead, just as the cost of war will be. No type of resistance is to be entered into lightly.

2 NUCLEAR PACIFISM

There are an increasing number of people who, though not pacifist, will not sanction the possession and use of *nuclear* weapons. The destruction is so vast and the effects so unpredictable that many feel their use would be suicidal. It has been said that nuclear pacifists are no different from 'total' pacifists, for they will always be open to blackmail by countries that have nuclear weapons.

That may be so in the present climate, but some nuclear pacifists look to new technology to produce a viable alternative that will be less destructive. It must be recognized, though, that this is very much faith in the unknown, and there are prices to be paid for this option, too:

The cost

1 Conventional offensive weapons are more expensive than nuclear, and need more manpower. The money and manpower could be spent on other things.
2 There is always the possibility of blackmail by the less scrupulous.
3 Hope is put on a technology to produce defensive weapons. This research is in its infancy, and its possibilities are still unknown.
4 Funding research into alternatives would be very costly.

3 NUCLEAR DETERRENCE

This is a third position, and has been the policy of the major powers for many years. Governments are, however, moving towards the manufacture of smaller nuclear tactical weapons. They are starting to think the unthinkable. With these more accurate weapons, designed for battlefield use, limited war is now a possibility. Christians have to face this change in policy when thinking about war. Is it something a Christian can contemplate? Or should Christians press for a move back to deterrence? Either way there is a price to be paid.

The cost

1 The amount spent on arms could be used for something else.
2 The immorality of threatening total destruction has to be considered.
3 The full consequences if there ever was a nuclear war, or an 'accident', would be horrendous.
4 Nuclear tactical weapons are less destructive – but more likely to be used. Christians are sometimes put in the position of backing the retention of larger, more destructive, weapons simply because their use is less likely. There is a cost to be borne in terms of conscience.

CHECK OUT THE BIBLE

● Look up Luke 14:28–33.
Jesus was always realistic about the cost involved in certain actions, and required others to 'count the cost' in the same way.

9.2 PRACTICAL OPTIONS

We have looked at the problems involved in this subject. We have also looked at the principles and now need to apply them. Below are a series of multiple-choice questions that will take you through the various decisions. This does not have to be a 'once-and-for-all' decision; you can make a decision in various stages. Neither are the choices always either/or; you can sometimes choose several options from one section.

For example, the series of choices you make may help you explain your position in a way something like the following: You decide that you are a nuclear pacifist (you will not use nuclear weapons) but feel that throwing all nuclear weapons away would be dangerous, so you propose a series of half-way measures that would keep the situation stable while you disarm slowly, replacing nuclear weapons with others.

(Make copies of the multiple choices and pin them around the room in sequence. Each person should then work through them, writing down the options they choose. It is possible to choose more than one in each section provided they do not conflict.)

DECISION TIME

Choice 1: The basic position

a. Total pacifism; no involvement in any form of coercion. No involvement in the police force or the courts.
b. Pacifism – but recognition of and involvement in the police force and the courts system.
c. Personally a pacifist, but agree that war is sometimes necessary even if you could not fight yourself.
d. Involvement in war but only under certain conditions (just war).
e. Nuclear pacifism – will use conventional weapons but not nuclear ones.
f. In favour of nuclear weapons as a deterrent.

Choice 2: The means of war

a. Non-violent resistance.
b. Conventional weapons (defensive).
c. Conventional weapons (offensive).
d. Biological weapons.
e. Chemical weapons.
f. Nuclear weapons.

Note: The distinction is made between defensive and offensive weapons but, of course, weapons of any type can be used in any way. The distinction is one of degree and intent, rather than one of nature.

Choice 3: The use of the weapons

a. As a last resort.
b. On humanitarian grounds only.
c. Purely defensive.
d. To defend justice.
e. To fight positively for justice.
f. To punish evil nations.

Choice 4: Some possible options

a. Making a nuclear-free corridor in the

81

middle of Europe between the two sides (an area of land where there are no nuclear weapons) so that the danger from a build-up of tension or a small skirmish is lessened.

b. Removing all battlefield nuclear weapons (small nuclear weapons that are designed for tactical targetting on troops or military equipment).

c. Targeting strategic (larger) nuclear weapons on military targets only (as far as possible, though it is recognized that this is extremely difficult).

d. Funding development of conventional (non-nuclear) defensive weapons, but being prepared to deploy conventional offensive weapons until these are developed.

e. Banning the use of biological and chemical weapons. Biological weapons are deadly in that they rely for their destructive power on the deliberate spread of disease. Chemical weapons destroy either people or the environment by the use of powerful chemicals. Forests can be sprayed with these chemicals or people gassed or burnt.

f. Funding the development of defensive policies. These are the sort of policies that make it clear they are not aggressive and therefore should not provoke the enemy.

g. Funding research into ways of verifying disarmament.

h. Working for the eventual replacement of nuclear weapons either totally or retaining only a minimal deterrent.

i. Reaching a 'no first strike' agreement (each country agrees not to use nuclear weapons first).

j. Funding research into civilian resistance.

k. Achieving a freeze on the production and testing of nuclear weapons (people will not buy untried weapons).

l. Funding research into anti-nuclear defence systems.

Choice 5: Nuclear deterrence

a. Minimum deterrence: enough to deter, but not enough to threaten the enemy into an arms build-up.

b. Maximum deterrence for security.

Choice 6: Disarmament

a. Multilateral disarmament, leading to a minimum level of arms being retained (all sides reducing arms).

b. Unilateral (one side going ahead and reducing arms without waiting for other nations).

c. Unilateral gesture (one side giving up a token number of weapons as a gesture to show their sincerity).

d. Multilateral disarmament, leading to total disarmament.

Don't despair!

These choices are limited; there are many other choices that may be made. You may feel that, at the end of this exercise, your decisions have made no difference – you still can't change the way things are. An exercise such as this, though, is meant only to help *you* decide where you stand. This may help you when you go to vote, and to understand the positions of the various political parties. Above all, you should be able to see that there are alternatives, there are choices; and when you are in a position to exercise your vote or be of some influence you will have thought about the issue.

10
THE FUTURE

10.1 WAGING PEACE

We are all familiar with the idea of waging war; we are less familiar with the idea of waging peace. People see peace as something that happens at the end of a war, something that most people are not involved in. In the Bible, peace is more than that, it is an aspect of life itself. It is wholeness and health, it is the situation when things are deeply sound and right.

People tend to see the issues of war and peace in terms of future decisions they hope they will never have to make. For the Christian the issues are more than that: the way you understand peace, and conflict of all kinds, will radically affect your whole lifestyle *now*. Christians believe that peace started at the cross when Jesus made it possible for people to find peace with God (see Ephesians 2:14–16). It then worked its way out into the community, breaking down the barriers between people (Galatians 3:28). Peace is one of the Christian facts of life, and a person's lifestyle should express that.

ACTIVITY

The peace market

Below is a 'peace market'; a variety of peace options that people can take up to incorporate into their lifestyles. This is 'preventative medicine', a way of life that avoids the wrong type of conflict but still faces up to the issues.

Some of these options for peace (see the list, 'Goods for the supermarket') are fairly easy to put into practice, others are very costly in terms of a person's lifestyle. Write these different options on pieces of paper and put them in a 'hat'. Each person should select (at random) one of these and spend a few minutes writing down the practical ways in which a person's lifestyle would change if they were to fulfil that option.

Alternatively, each person can talk for about two minutes to the rest of the group about their option, saying what they think it would cost in terms of time, effort and change of lifestyle.

When everyone has a fairly clear idea about what each option would entail, pin the various pieces of paper around the wall. Everybody should go around the room and write on each of the options what they would estimate the price to be in terms of a person's way of life – saying how much it would cost them in effort. To do this they will need to use the scale of values below:

VALUES

1 = Easy
5 = Not much effort
10 = Involves a bit of work/time
20 = Fairly hard work
50 = Hard work
75 = Time-consuming, involves a change in lifestyle
100 = Total commitment; a complete change in lifestyle

When everyone has been around the room, go through the different papers and see if the group can settle on an agreed value for each option. (You may wish to divide up the 'Goods for the supermarket' among small groups, in order to speed up the process.)

Put the pieces of paper back up on the wall and go 'shopping'. Each person should go around and select the things they think they can do for peace, writing them down on a piece of paper if necessary, thinking carefully about the effect it will have on *their* lives.

Think about it . . .

Many people, not only Christians, want to contribute to 'peace', but are not sure what they can do. Some items on the list below may help you decide how to contribute.

Working for peace is not optional for the Christian; all Christians are called to be peacemakers, though what they do may vary. All Christians are told to pray for their leaders, though only some are called into politics. All Christians are called to work for peace, though only some are called to be full-time evangelists.

GOODS FOR THE SUPERMARKET

1 Pray for people in government and all those who are involved in negotiations.
2 Make your own relationships peaceful. This doesn't mean a false avoidance of conflict, but seeking to work through conflicts to a restoration of relationships.
3 Strive for justice and peace within your own community. Social justice at local level is preventative work and demonstrates the love of God in action. Start with small, specific items: support local schemes that help the underpriviledged; befriend lonely people at school or work.
4 Encourage your MP. Write to your local MP about relevant situations. He/

she needs to know that Christian young people notice, and care about, what is happening in the world.
5 Find out about other countries, particularly countries that are labelled as 'enemies', so that you can pray and work in an informed way. Don't put off doing things just because you think you can't make any difference. Don't rely on stereotypes for your understanding of others.
6 Encourage and support those who work for freedom and order. People who are in 'front-line' jobs – in the police, army or in politics – need to know they are doing a worthwhile job, and need encouragement.
7 Free someone else's time to work for peace. Christians are meant to act as a body. Actively working for peace may not be *your* 'calling' but you can provide someone else with the time to read, or act for peace, by taking some of their workload or doing things practically for them.
8 If you are a Christian make sure that you maintain your own hope in Christ.

The problems may look massive but God is bigger still. Do not neglect worship, prayer and Bible study, as a true understanding of peace will come out of these things.

9 Live more simply, give the money you save to those in need, and encourage others to do the same. In this way you will help reduce the exploitation of others.

10 Remind yourself regularly of the plight of the poor, the cruelty of war and the tyranny of oppression so that you do not forget that for some people these are daily realities. But always balance this with hope.

11 Look at the way your life is organized and see if you can make it less competitive and less conflict-orientated.

12 Make the effort to get out into the countryside, so that you can begin to feel more responsible for creation. Wherever possible, make your own contribution to its conservation and protection.

13 Read about war and peace and keep yourself informed.

14 Join an organization for peace, not necessarily a pacifist one.

15 Educate others as well as yourself, talk about these issues with others. If possible, put on a display of information at church or school.

16 Think about your own future involvement in politics. It may be an area you can work in either on a local or a national scale.

17 If you are a Christian, support evangelism. The gospel is one of peace and as it spreads so peace spreads.

18 Think very carefully about what job you do. It is better to ask questions beforehand than find yourself in a difficult position afterwards.

19 Stand firm beside your friends, even if they come to a different decision from you over this question.

20 Think carefully about joining the armed forces. It is better to sort out your position on war before you enter the forces than afterwards. The forces need peacemakers too, and joining can be an expression of your concern for peace.

When each person has made their list of things they feel they could do, share these with others if that is appropriate.

Think about it . . .

Most people feel helpless over issues such as war and peace, but we can do something about our own attitudes. Government can only start wars based on hatred and greed if hatred and greed are found in the general population. We tend to have an 'all or nothing' approach to this subject, thinking that because we can't abolish war it isn't worth doing anything. The Bible makes it clear that people should get on and work where they can, healing what they can and preventing what evil they can.

Look up these verses:

- John 16:33
- Philippians 4:6–7

Peace is a personal reality for the Christian, but we cannot expect the same peace in the world of politics. Any peace that people know in this world will be a very fragile affair indeed.

10.2 HOPE

We have spent a lot of time looking at this difficult and often depressing subject. One thing ought to be clear, particularly to the Christian: there is hope. Hope, like peace and love, is a word we frequently use but seldom stop to think about. This final session will be spent looking at the biblical concept of hope, and its practical implications.

ACTIVITY ONE

Hope = certainty
Copy the following list on to pieces of paper and put them face down on the floor.

HOPES

1 I hope I can go on holiday this year
2 I hope I can go to see a film this weekend
3 I hope the sun rises tomorrow
4 I hope I get a job when I leave school/college
5 I hope I get married to someone extremely rich and very handsome/beautiful
6 I hope the world becomes a better place to live in
7 I hope I pass my exams
8 I hope I become queen
9 I hope it doesn't rain tomorrow
10 I hope I get a new bike
11 I hope wars will stop
12 I hope I get some sleep tonight
13 I hope I get a pay rise
14 I hope I get up in time for work/school
15 I hope I haven't missed the bus

The following descriptions should then be written on separate pieces of paper, of a different colour from the first list, and put face down on the floor:

DESCRIPTIONS

1 A baby
2 The Prime Minister
3 The Queen
4 A schoolboy
5 A television personality
6 A scientist
7 A millionaire
8 A politician
9 The President of the USA
10 A housewife
11 A shopkeeper
12 A doctor
13 A factory worker
14 A cleaner
15 God

(Please add to or subtract from these lists so that the number of items matches the number of people in your group.)

Members of the group should select two pieces of paper, one of each colour, and decide whether the person they have selected could bring about the event they have hope for; was the 'hope' in any way feasible for that person? Use the scale below to vote on how likely it is that these events will happen.

VOTING SCALE

1 Definitely impossible
2 Most unlikely
3 Not very likely
4 Maybe
5 Likely
6 Fairly certain
7 Definite

For example

Description: The Queen

Hope: I hope I get a new bike.

Vote: Definite – she can afford it.

NEW BIKE

H.M
THE QUEEN

Think about it . . .

1 Were some hopes possible because the events were in the control of the person selected?

2 Were some hopes impossible because of the nature of the hope?

Think carefully; is hope a certainty because of the type of things you hope for (things that are easy to fulfil), or is it the person behind the hope that makes it certain? For example, if my hope is to go to some distant island for a holiday, and I am a schoolgirl, it is most unlikely that I will be able to go. I probably couldn't afford it and school commitments might stop me. In this case I am stopped both by the nature of the hope and the scope of who I am. If, on the other hand I am a millionaire, it is likely that I can go on such a holiday; it is within my scope.

In the Bible there is hope; there is hope that one day Jesus will come again and all war will cease. There is also hope in the fact that God is still involved and active in his world, and we can work in partnership with him. What sort of vote would you give this hope on the voting scale?

We often hope for things that are beyond our control and because of that we have to rely on others, or circumstances, to bring them about. This makes hope seem a bit uncertain because we can't be sure our hopes will come true. Our hopes are often too big for either us or others to put into action.

BIBLICAL HOPE

In the Bible hope is different.

- *Firstly, hope is certain* because hope is grounded in God and nothing is too big for him.

- *Secondly, hope involves a relationship* of quiet trust. You put your faith only in people you trust. Hope can only be encouraged if you believe not only that God *can* save, but also that he is *willing* to. Hope comes from a relationship of love.

- *Thirdly, hope faces the facts.* Hope is not blind; it faces reality. Hope looks evil in the eye and says not only *will* good eventually triumph, but it already *has* triumphed. Hope recognizes the full force of evil and still says God has defeated it – a fact that he will one day make obvious to everyone.

- *Fourthly, hope looks to the past.* In our culture we always look to the future, often at the expense of the present. In the Bible, hope looks to the past and sees that God can be trusted because of his past record, and then lives in the present trusting God for the future.

- *Lastly, Christian hope is certain to be fulfilled, because God is all-powerful and all-loving.* That doesn't mean he will give us a trouble-free life, but it does mean that God is present and active in even the darkest situation and that he will ultimately save. 'Ultimately' may seem a long way off. Christians believe that in the end all war will cease because God will intervene to end all evil. God is not passive until then but is closely involved in our world, actively working within history.

- Read Isaiah chapter 40
This reading helps us to get a true perspective on the might of God.

ACTIVITY TWO

Comparison

Stand three people side by side: one short, one medium height and one tall. The medium height person looks tall compared with the shortest person until you put them both against the tallest person. Height, like many other things in life, is a matter of comparison.

Think about it . . .

We spend our lives making comparisons; we compare our looks, our intelligence, our clothes and our partners. For the Christian there is a constant comparison going on. For the Christian everything should be measured not only by the standards of God, but also by God himself. Problems often look immense, and so they are in comparison with our capabilities. What Christians have to do is measure the size of the problem against God's ability – not their own. It is a matter of looking at God before looking at the problem; it is keeping problems in their proper perspective.

Look up the following passages in the Bible:

- Hebrews 11:1
- Romans 4:18

Hope is the ability to see with a vision that other people do not have. When a situation looks overwhelming hope says that God is in control. Hope looks at a different set of realities and lives in the light of them. Christians need to train themselves to constantly 'see' this invisible set of realities and live lives that reflect them. If Christians know that good is stronger than evil, then that knowledge, or hope, should have practical results in their lives. It is no use talking about qualities such as love, peace and hope if our own lives are full of frantic activity, selfishness and worry! Christians need to present to others a living demonstration of the alternative.

As a group, share with each other the things about war and pacifism that you find difficult. What is there about the Christian message that helps us deal with those difficulties?

If you are a Christian, remember this: **hope is not just for the good times**. Hope, like love, is only valid when it has really been tested. We can all hope when things are going well; that isn't real hope, that's just wishful thinking. Real hope is when we can say with Habakkuk:

'Though the fig tree does not bud
    and there are no grapes on the vines,
though the olive crop fails
    and the fields produce no food,
though there are no sheep in the pen
    and no cattle in the stalls,
yet I will rejoice in the Lord,
    I will be joyful in God my Saviour.'
(Habakkuk 3:17–18).

BOOKS ON WAR AND PACIFISM

Peace in Our Time, D Atkinson, IVP

Pacifism and War, O Barclay (ed), IVP

Who are the Peacemakers? J Barrs, Crossway Books

The Cross and the Bomb, F Bridger, Mowbray

Does the Bible teach Pacifism? R E D Clark, Fellowship of Reconciliation

Dropping the Bomb, J Gladwin (ed), Hodder and Stoughton

Christianity and War in a Nuclear Age, R Harries, Mowbray

The Nuclear Age, ed Brenda Lealman, Christian Education Movement

The Church and the Bomb, The report of a working party under the chairmanship of the Bishop of Salisbury, Hodder and Stoughton

Nuclear Holocaust and Christian Hope, R J Sider and R K Taylor, Hodder and Stoughton

Religion and Social Justice, John St John, Religious and Moral Education Press

THE PHILIPPINES:
Witness to the people's power

(This article is included as it illustrates a recent situation where Christians have successfully, and peacefully, resisted a corrupt Government. It raises many issues, and may be useful to refer to from time to time throughout this study.)

'I'm sure no one ever thought it could happen. It was the people who did it.' Such was Cory Aquino's comment on her electoral victory over President Marcos in late February.

The non-violent 'democratic revolution' in the Philippines has drawn the world's attention and admiration. It has become a sign of hope for resistance movements, especially those with Christian motivation, in many other countries under oppressive regimes. One Christian caught up in the movement of 'people power' in the Philippines was American Mac Bradshaw, Associate Director of Evangelism and Development in the Manila-based Field Development Office of *World Vision*, a Christian aid and development agency.

Third Way met Mac Bradshaw and heard his eyewitness account of events and his hopes for the future.

Could you describe to us the role of the church in the Philippine revolution?

Let's start with the high point when Minister Enrile and General Ramos had gone into Camp Aguinaldo and really declared the beginning of the revolution. That was a period of intense danger, because of the vastly superior power that the President had at his disposal and the fact that the President had discovered the coup. Cardinal Sin came on *Radio Veritas* and asked everybody to go to Camp Aguinaldo and Camp Crame and protect Ramos and Enrile from the government forces, and the people went. It was a spontaneous movement in that direction. My own family, although we were foreigners, just sensed that need to be there, and went too.

There'd been a lot of preparation. That's shown by the fact that the Cardinal could ask and the whole nation would respond, in fact at one point a million and a half or two million ended up there. I think the Cardinal should at least be recommended for the *Nobel Peace Prize* for that.

I don't want to credit just the political preparations of the Catholic Church, but the deep prayer, faith and trust in God which prepared a nation to be ready, to sacrifice their lives for freedom and to do it peacefully. Now underneath this I would say that there is a tremendous spiritual renewal going on in the Catholic Church in the Philippines and I speak at this point from the perspective of an evangelical. Let me give you an example. Recently a correspondent interviewed the number three leader in the Communist Party who is a Catholic priest, and he said that the Communist Party has to play its cards within the next two years. There were several reasons given as to why it was so necessary for them to move now and one of them was the rapid advance of the Catholic charismatic renewal all over the countryside.

As to the evangelical churches, there is a vibrant element in the evangelical church. The Protestant church is quite small – 8–10 per cent. The evangelicals had been using Romans 13 all through as an excuse not to get involved or to stay with the Marcos government; but there is a group called ISACC, the *Institute for Studies in Asian Church and Culture*, which broke with this a long time ago and accurately analysed the situation of injustice and oppression in the country far ahead of any of the

93

other evangelical groups. They were very instrumental in the formation of a group called KONFES that played a very active part in the revolution.

Even I in the weeks preceeding the election was praying for the physical survival of Cory Aquino because deep down I could not believe that she would be able to preserve her life – and yet at the end of it we have a bloodless revolution. What do you think accounts for that?

I remember reading or hearing that Napoleon at Elba, when he was reflecting what had happened to him, said, 'There was a hand moving in Europe which I did not see'. I think that's what we have to say about the Philippines: there was a hand moving which no one could have predicted or that no one could explain. Most people who were involved in the movement to overthrow Marcos can attest to miracles, as I can in my family. My children were between the two camps where all the people were gathered (the camps are just over the road from each other). Now we had a shift system with our *Covenant Community* and Rhoda and I were on the 8.00 to 12.00 shift. But my oldest son Todd had the morning shift and that was the most dangerous time because the crowds did thin out towards daybreak. On the day when Marcos' troops were expected to attack, there were only 40 of them guarding a very key route that went right into the gate of Camp Crame. They could hear the tanks coming, and *Radio Veritas* said that one group off the street had been gassed with tear gas. Then they saw the troops coming into their street with shields and truncheons and he said that they were kneeling down and really expected to die. He got so sick that he was just about to throw up. But when the troops came closer, they just stopped and turned back. One of the stories is that when the tear gas was used, the wind shifted and blew it back on the troops, which led the colonel to say, 'The hand of God is here', and he surrendered. Then the daylight came and the helicopters came in and instead of bombing, they surrendered.

All over the place people can say that there was no mastermind behind any of it, and yet all of these unusual incidents were orchestrated into one force that was irresistibly victorious. The people were ready to die and they expected to die. There was much fear, but yet nevertheless, no one broke ranks and started throwing stones. They gave the troops flowers, they gave them food, they brought water to the tanks, and simply by that love they would not let the troops move in or fire.

The Catholic Church's commitment to change in the Philippines goes back a number of years. It's difficult quite to see the game that Cardinal Sin was playing, because on the one hand he would not commit himself to either side before the election and yet at the same time he was encouraging the reform movement in the military, encouraging Cory Aquino to stand, putting together that remarkable partnership between her and her running mate Salvador Laurel, and working to create an environment where the protection of the integrity of the ballot was extremely important. These are not neutral acts, are they?

Well, the key thing was *Namfrel* which is the poll watching body. *Namfrel* sought to be a neutral body, just making sure that the ballot boxes were not tampered with and watching the counting. The Cardinal backed this neutral body, but on the other hand it would not have been necessary to have such a body if the ruling party and the government was honest – so in a sense it wouldn't have existed unless it was assumed that the government was going to be dishonest. During the elections the Bishops in general endorsed the integrity of *Namfrel* and therefore when the *Namfrel* poll counts determined that Mrs Aquino was winning, then most of the Bishops said, 'We believe this is the voice of the people'.

Of course the Catholic radio station was also absolutely believable. The second one I would recommend for the *Nobel Peace Prize* is June Keithly, the announcer on *Radio Veritas*. She was the channel through whom Ramos' and Enrile's orders to the troops went, in fact all communication went through *Veritas*. Even when the transmitter was blown up and the station was off the air, she went out and looked for a radio station, she had to find it herself and nobody knew where she was. At one point she said, 'If anyone knows where I am get some help over here right away'.

The most outstanding significance to me, is that this is an occasion where a nation has proved that Jesus' way really works; 'Blessed are the peacemakers'.

Time Magazine had a headline: 'Now for the hard part', and in many ways that's true. You have a country which has been stripped of some of its wealth, in terrible disarray. How would you see the future of the Philippines?

First of all I would say this spiritual resurgence will probably continue and multiply many times over. Secondly, I believe that the people of the Philippines own this revolution, it's theirs and nothing can take it away. Therefore, this 'praying people power' will continue to give its support to the new government. When I left, the *Christian Covenant Community* which I belong to was preparing to offer voluntary help and expertise to the new departments which are just being reorganised and trying to get back on their feet. This kind of support and trust in Mrs Aquino and the new government is going to go a long way towards a successful follow up to the revolution.

When you say that the revolution is solely that of the Philippines people, you are obviously making a reference to President Reagan. It seems that he has pointed to his role in the Philippines and in Haiti to suggest that he is a good supporter of human rights. And yet in the same breath he wanted to raise money for the contras in Nicaragua.

It was very disappointing to us that he didn't see long before he did what was happening. I feel he was dragged in reluctantly and did not come in wholeheartedly. I guess he did play a part, but he didn't really impress the people of the Philippines that he was the saviour. I don't give him credit for being a great human rights advocate at this point.

Talking about the reaction of the evangelical church in the prerevolutionary time, you were saying part of the church retreated behind Romans 13. Could you amplify that?

Romans 13 just led to a kind of paralysis, whereas friends of mine in the Catholic Church were also citing Revelation 13, which indicates that there is a certain point at which the authority of a ruler comes from the kingdom of darkness rather than from the kingdom of light. But the evangelicals weren't making those kind of distinctions. The leader of the *Council of Evangelical Churches*, right up to the end, was saying, 'If we believe that the elections were rigged then let's bring the case to the courts' – ie assuming that you could still get a fair trial when everything else had been unfair. But *Diliman Bible Church*, just one small church, took a stand for justice and righteousness and really came out for the opposition very early in the game. They are an outstanding example of evangelicals who blazed the trail. ISACC and KONFES are another example of people who analysed the situation far in advance and took a stand.

Far East Broadcasting Company, the evangelical radio station, tried to be so neutral that it was a great disappointment to the people from ISACC and KONFES. But when Ramos and Enrile went into Camp Aguinaldo the station immediately came to their aid.

Presumably in ceasing to be neutral FEBC was putting itself at great risk, because at the early stage there was no guarantee that Ramos and Enrile would win.

That's true. And also *Radio Veritas* when it did go off the air told its audience to switch to FEBC. In fact *Radio Veritas* sent a microwave unit to FEBC so that FEBC would be in touch with the camp and all that was going on in different parts of the city and relay messages in and out.

I think the thing that is really changing the evangelical world is the emergence of wholistic ministry in which the Christian's role in the whole life of the nation and in evangelism are seen as equally valid. In *World Vision Philippines* I can see that this concept of the Kingdom of God, the kingdom which is going to come but which is already manifesting itself in ordinary life, is changing the way that *World Vision* does its ministry.

What is your hope for tomorrow?

I feel this could be one of the hinges of history as regards the spread of the gospel in Asia. This, I feel, is going to be one of the places where there will be a remarkable turning to the Lord and that the Filipinos will be carriers of the gospel in a very unusual way. I think this is the destiny of the country and many of us have expected this for a long time.

Is that because you have combined the renewal of the spirit in the churches with a commitment to participation in the whole of society?

Yes, and a love for the word of God and a love for Jesus. And because the spirit of God is working in such a way as to work with what's there, not to discard what's there. So these events seem to me to be setting the stage for something very exciting which we all need to watch. And I think evangelical Christianity has a real part in that it is an instrument to introduce these ideas of wholistic ministry.

This article appeared in the June 1986 issue of *Third Way*, and is reproduced by kind permission.

Third Way seeks to provide a biblical perspective on politics, social ethics and cultural affairs in the contemporary world.

Further details and subscription rates: *Third Way*, 37 Elm Road, New Malden, Surrey KT3 3HB.